I Remember Your Name in the Night

THINKING ABOUT DEATH

Donagh O'Shea

DOMINICAN PUBLICATIONS
TWENTY-THIRD PUBLICATIONS

First published (1997) by
Dominican Publications
42 Parnell Square
Dublin 1

and

Twenty-Third Publications
P.O. Box 180, 185 Willow Street
Mystic CT 06355

ISBN 1-871552-58-3 (Dominican Publications)
ISBN 0-89622-718-9 (Twenty-Third Publications)

British Library Cataloguing in Publication Data.
A catalogue record for this book is available from
the British Library.

Printed in the United States of America.

Library of Congress Catalog Card Number 96-61628

Contents

Acknowledgements

I am deeply grateful to Vivian Boland, Paul Murray, Eppie Brasil and Maria Zamora who read the manuscript and made many valuable suggestions; also to Martin Cogan of Rollebon Press for his constant encouragement and his generous permission to reprint most of the material of this book.

Introduction

Whichever way the world turns, whatever gods are born or die, whatever thoughts are in or out of season, death remains the eternal question hanging over our life. We no longer expect a simple answer to its mystery – I mean an answer that can be handed to us, leaving us unchanged – but we would like to know where to look, and how to look at that great question without falsifying it or deluding ourselves.

A friend said to me, 'I will be very surprised if there is anything after death'. On reflection I think this better than the cocksureness that sees only smooth continuity ahead, with no break, no crisis, no surprise. At least my friend promises to have the good grace to be surprised by the resurrection. We can explain to ourselves, like the reasonable Polonius, 'All who live must die,' but beyond that we cannot give ourselves a satisfactory account of death. We could certainly offer suggestions for redesigning this existence of ours, 'this house,' as Tauler called it; but even the most avant-garde house designer has to admit defeat when the house falls down.

In antiquity, the Christian cult of the tombs and relics of the martyrs filled educated pagans with horror. 'You have filled the whole world with tombs and sepulchres,' wrote Julian the Apostate. Jews and pagans alike buried their dead outside the city, away from places of habitation. This separation reflected the unbridgeable chasm they saw between the living and the dead. Christians, with their cult of the dead, seemed to be erasing the structure of existence itself; such was the impact of their belief in the closeness of the beyond.

Today, the whole ground of experience has moved, even moved to the opposite. I looked in a dictionary of Christian spirituality for an article on 'Death'. There was only one – and

that was on the 'Death of God'! Its companion volume, a new
dictionary of Christian theology, offered exactly the same fare.
This is astonishing when you consider that the central icon of the
Christian faith is the cross of Christ. He 'was found in human
form and became obedient unto death,' but the human form in
those dictionaries does not appear to be subject to death at all!

If there is no resurrection, St Paul said, our faith is in vain.
Equally, if there is no death, there is no resurrection. Or, to put
it on a scale, the more we avoid the thought of death, the more
meaningless it becomes to speak of resurrection – and the more
absurd death itself becomes.

Is it correct to remain silent, like those editors? To do so, I
think, would be to see death only as a brute fact, and we cannot
live humanly with brute facts; we have to see them humanly, and
this makes them human facts. We cannot give an account of
death, and yet we cannot leave the subject alone.

When our life enters the season for dying, we will know death
directly. It will be a new experience then, not a second-hand one:
death is the one experience whose purity we will never destroy.
If we have lived all our lives on other people's ideas and through
other people's experiences, our death at least will be our own. In
other words, if we have spent all our lives avoiding direct
experience, now at last it will fill our horizon completely. And
if we have always thought it bad form to mention death, now at
the end it will be a subject of passionate interest.

The first three chapters of this book are about leave-taking
and death in the ordinary sense of the word. The remaining three
are about another kind of dying that we have to do every day:
dying to the ego, the fictional self. The most delusive of all egos
is the religious one. Unlike the secular ego, it projects its falsity
to infinity, constructing not only a false living and dying, but a
false heaven beyond, inhabited by a false god. Getting to
understand the ways of the ego and striving to live beyond them
– that is, dying to the ego, 'dying to oneself' – is the homework
we have to do for death. Meditation is a privileged 'place' in
which to follow this dying; it can open the mind and heart to the

way of emptiness: a deeper way of living.

Each chapter is divided into about a dozen short sections. Each section stands by itself. This is because I love beginnings and ends, and I wanted to have as many as possible – sixty or seventy little births and deaths! It is also a convenience for busy readers: I mean readers who are busy with things other than reading!

ONE

Knowing Death to the Bone

Mac

She was 100½ years old at the time (the half becomes important in extreme old age as in extreme youth). I was exactly half her age, and we had arranged to meet in the afternoon. When we sat down together she leaned over and whispered, 'I hope people won't get the wrong idea about this!' The age of romance is never over! She is known to all as Mac, a valorous woman, nowhere near dead, and she is now 101¾. When her younger sister died her friends were worried that this would shatter the old lady, and they scarcely knew how to break the news to her. During the funeral they were a great support, even in a physical sense, offering numerous arms to lean on. She did bravely, and when they brought her home and she was hanging up her coat, she said, 'We had a great day!'

I often try to think of that great day that lies ahead of everyone; who doesn't? Some think about it, some try not to think about it (which is just another way of thinking about it). Prospero in *The Tempest* was one who planned to think much about it, but not too much. I will 'retire me to Milan (he said) where every third thought shall be my grave.' Someone remarked that for an old man this was about the right proportion.

The last of the three ages (youth, middle age and 'you're looking well!') is probably no more secure against wishful thinking than the other two; but we cannot all hope to live to be 101¾; probably we will have died long before. It is not too soon, and it is not at all morbid, to cast a thought on death.

Death is the constant companion of life. It gives our life a particular length, obviously. A little less obviously it gives it a particular quality: a poignancy, a once-for-all feeling, a salty taste – for tears are never far away. This is something, we know, that can be prized, not hated. We can imagine how dreadful life would be if we could not die. Do I want to live till the day when I have to say, 'I have lived too long?' 'Too long' (too anything) means something is wrong. I should die a little before that day. I know I have no choice in the matter, but I have to think right about it: death is not the worst possible prospect; it would be worse if I lived to say 'I have lived too long.' For heaven's sake, even a football match that went on too long would be intolerable! It is the final whistle that enlivens the whole game. It does this by *defining* it, that is, putting limits to it. The end is constantly present to each player throughout the match, and it prevents him from falling down with boredom.

'This medicine is good for you, so just swallow it!' We did, but we didn't like it. Death is good for you (you can say to yourself), but you don't have to like it! Death is reasonable, but it would be unreasonable to expect that we should approach it with cold reason as if it were some object outside us. Think of the restlessness, the doubts, the fears we had during the other turning points on our journey – childhood, adolescence, midlife – and we took them as normal (or, at least, there was no shortage of advisers to tell us that that was how we ought to take them). Why shouldn't we go through some rough weather at the final turning point? When the two-year-old is kicking and screaming we just say, 'He (or she) is going through a difficult stage,' and everyone understands. When I am a hundred and two why shouldn't I expect equal understanding, especially from myself, now that I have reached the age of reason? After all, it will be my first time to die. So let me not panic if I shake a bit already at the thought of it. It's normal! A two-year-old doesn't regard the day as a write-off just because he or she did a bit of screaming and kicking. Every day, for them, is a great day. Why should it be different for us?

Right, Mac?

Passing away

There has always been a reluctance, it seems, to talk directly about death. People have been saying that ours is the first age in which it has become the great unmentionable. This is not true. A look at the history of the word 'death' will tell you. Etymologists say that the word 'to die' was borrowed from Old Norse. It may seem strange that English should have to borrow a word for what is a universal occurrence, but it is normal for 'die' words to slip their meaning faster than other words, and therefore to need constant replacing. From Old English, 'steorfan' and 'sweltan', both of which mean 'to die', have come down to us in attenuated forms as 'starve' and 'swelter'. Likewise 'cwelan' ('to kill') has come down to us as 'quell'. You sense an unease. Euphemisms like 'passing away' and 'falling asleep' are not such new inventions; and at the other extreme (an extreme always calls out its opposite) there is the vulgar way of referring to death: 'snuffing it', and so on. There is some kind of denial built into this too: violence is always a denial. To talk of 'stiffs', for example, is to brutalise death so far that it seems foreign to us.

The other great unmentionable has been sex. But now, as a reaction, it is mentioned with brutish persistence; there is a kind of flaunting that looks like nothing but revenge on the past. The expressions for pregnancy, likewise, pass at both sides of the reality itself: the vulgar and the euphemistic. In Italian, a woman is said to be 'in an interesting condition'. It all goes to show that it is very hard to look straight at some things.

Why is it difficult to look straight at death? What do we see when we look? The end. But we don't want our life to end, so we don't want to look. The end puts everything in question. The end means that I can no longer project into the future: it is the end of all procrastination. My idea of who I am includes many fictional notions of who I will be, many big and small plans – to fix that window, to finish some projects, 'to become a better person' – but the thought of death puts paid to them all, big and small. The end means a cataclysmic now! – a vivid here and now, as when you are involved in an accident.

That is what the thought of death does to us, but do we know anything about the reality? In a strict sense, no, because we are still alive. But many of us have seen others die, and all of us have known people who died later. It is common experience that a dying person has no difficulty in talking about death, while the relatives are rigid with inhibition. I once saw an old man become really angry (it was one of the few times in his life, it seems) when a nephew tried to pretend that death was nowhere near. 'That's only stupid talk!' he said, 'I'm dying!' It seems that people who are dying can cope better with death than the rest of us who are only watching it or thinking about it. As we watch, we have to admit: it doesn't seem to be so bad when a person gets on with it.

This stands to reason. When we are in a situation we have the resources to cope with it, otherwise we don't. In our bodies, it seems, we know something about death that we don't know in our minds. 'My grace is sufficient for you.' Grace doesn't keep; it is given for now, not for cold storage. When death comes we will receive the grace of death. Look back on your life: you always received the grace of the moment but never a future instalment!

The old man on his deathbed knew it first, and reassured us with his eyes. He didn't 'pass away' euphemistically; he died fair and square.

Knowing death to the bone

You look up at the sun and it looks motionless in the sky; you can even show, if you have a flair for astronomy, that it doesn't move. Yet by evening it is shining through a different window of your house. Your house, too, is stationary; from morning till evening it never moves; yet by evening everything is different. Things ought to be the same as before, yet the whole ground of everything has shifted. This is how age comes upon us.

There is some security, however, in the fact that we are all ageing together, that all our friends are with us ... until a few of them die. Some time after the funeral there is the shock of realisation that their life has stopped. Even if I live for another thirty years, you say, I will never hear her voice or his voice again. The only memories I will have, thirty years from now, are the ones I have now; nothing will ever be added. Their life is 'cut off from the loom,' as Isaiah said with such terrible accuracy. Everything they knew and said, everything they felt, everything they dreamed about and longed for is past. We have an urge to store up every memory we have of them, to make collections, to ask others.... It is all a proof, as if proof were needed, that their story is finished. It is all over, and that is why even the small details have become precious.

Now, look carefully. Whose life are you gathering up? Whose are these fragments? Are they not yours, just as much as your friend's? They are what you had in common. Your dead friend was the guarantor of your existence, not of your mere existence but of the fact that you lived meaningfully. Now that he or she is gone, your existence is no longer as solid as before; the reality of your past is in question. Their life has stopped and you are moving on. They mark the difference between past and present with awesome clarity. If you have been identifying yourself with your past, then that past has fallen to pieces with the death of your friend. So in your desperation you gather up its fragments.

Death forces depth on us. We cannot look back unhesitatingly at our past and say, 'that's me.' Our past is forever dying and passing into the present. Some part of it dies every time a friend or one of our family dies. It dies and disappears. In a sense, not only the Lord's tomb but every tomb is empty. 'Why do you look for the living among the dead ... ? He is not here.' Neither are we; we do not exist in the past. Death constrains us to take the whole meaning of our life in our hands now, to look to the present. 'He is not here; he is risen. Come and see the place where he lay.' Check out the tomb, check out the past. It does not contain your friend. Nor you. Your friend is nowhere if not risen. And you too: you are nowhere if not risen from the past.

Meanwhile our own death lies in the future. It is the big Stop sign up ahead.... To all appearances we will be annihilated, and our friends will gather the fragments of what we had in common with them; then they will have to move on: 'they closed the tomb and all withdrew.' The sun will shine through other windows.

How simple it is for the animals! They come and go, without needing to read or write about it! Yeats wrote:

> Nor dread nor hope attend
> A dying animal;
> A man awaits his end
> Dreading and hoping all....

But I still don't envy them, do you? Yes, a terrible knowledge has been released in us, the knowledge of death; but without it we could not penetrate to any extent the mystery of life. Death is the dark valley, life is the mountain that rises above it. Without the valley there is no mountain. Animals run on level ground; but we human creatures know the heights and the depths. We know life and death from the inside; we know them to the bone.

Wakes and funerals

My father remembered staying up all night, as a young man, to 'wake' a neighbour who had died and been buried in America. The wake began like any other, but of course without the corpse. As the small hours passed, however, many felt that it was not a notable success. An old man leaned over to my father and said quite seriously, 'I tell you, there's nothing like a corpse to put a bit of life into a wake!'

It was in the spirit of the old-fashioned Irish wake: death domesticated; 'he's a lovely corpse, God bless him; that last holiday did him the world of good.' Strange! – but much better than making death an obscenity. Obscene: *ob-scena*, what is 'off-stage', behind the curtains. Sex used to be the great obscenity, now (but not for the first time) it is death. A friend told me of a depressing cremation he had witnessed. The dead person had been an unbeliever, and the readings and 'prayers' (or good

wishes, or whatever) were picked clean of any religious suggestions, so as not to be offensive to pagan ears. There were only five
people present. It was not a memorial but an attempt to forget,
or perhaps an acknowledgement that they had already forgotten.
It was entirely 'inconclusive,' my friend said; nothing was
attempted, and so nothing was concluded.

Wakes and funerals have multiple layers of meaning. At the
most practical level, the purpose is to dispose of the body in a
dignified way. At the religious level, it is to pray for the dead, and
to affirm the community's hope for the resurrection. At the
psychological level it is to convince those left behind that the
person really is dead. The psyche automatically protects itself
against too much pain, just as the hands automatically protect
the head. It does this by not fully believing at once that death has
visited the house. This merciful numbness lasts a short time; if
it continues, however, it becomes a perilous denial of the truth.
The psychological purpose of the funeral rites is to bring the
bereaved to a gradual acceptance of the painful truth, while
surrounding them with the love and support of the whole
community – just as the whole body concentrates on the
wounded part.

I met a woman whose brother had died in Australia and been
buried there. At home in Ireland the family had Masses said for
him, and while they attended other Masses they did not in fact
attend any of those Masses; they had no special Mass, then, that
might have been something like a funeral Mass. As the months
went by, she began to have a fixed idea (which she knew to be
absurd, but it would not leave her) that her brother had taken up
residence in a derelict house that the family owned. We had a
special Requiem Mass, attended by the whole family, and she
was able to take leave of her brother; in my friend's language, she
was able to 'conclude'. We have to take proper leave of the dead.
A ghost is a dead person to whom no one has said a proper
goodbye. In a world where death is become an obscenity, there
must be many of them around.

We also need a focus for our grief: a last resting place. It is a resting place not only for the dead, but for ourselves. To focus our grief is to be able to limit and control it. There is a far greater grief for families who have not been able to bury their dead; it all remains in the mind. Is it possible that sometimes a preference for cremation is avoidance of the reality of death? There is a big difference between a movable urn and a fixed resting place. People have their own preferences; mine is for burial. I want my last contribution to this world (which has fed me all my life) to be fertilisation of the earth rather than pollution of the atmosphere.

What is your soul?

Something white inside that blackens when you sin…. We soon abandoned that idea of the soul. But what is it now, at the age of twenty or forty or eighty? It loses its colour, for one thing – I mean white and black equally – and so it becomes a sort of colourless bubble (of uncertain whereabouts), till one day perhaps it goes 'pop!' or, more likely, it gets a slow puncture and dies that way.

In all sanity what is it? Or is it an 'it' at all? Many a thing that we refer to as 'it' is not an 'it' at all; for instance when we say, 'It is raining,' what is this 'it' that is said to be raining? 'The rain is raining all around / It falls on field and tree,' wrote Robert Louis Stevenson, but that was playful verse for children. And the clown in *Twelfth Night* who sang, 'The rain it raineth every day,' was just being a proper clown. What is rain apart from the raining? In Italian there is no sign of any 'it' that rains, and this is not because they have a better climate in Italy; it is because the structure of their language is different. English grammar inserts the word 'it', but it does not refer to a thing. Likewise the word 'soul' does not refer to a thing. But then what does it refer to?

Think of it this way: if you switch on the radio and listen to a foreign language (a really foreign one, in which you cannot guess the meaning of even one word) you have the experience of hearing everything and yet nothing. You have to admit that you are hearing every sound; there is nothing wrong with your hearing, and speakers on radio are usually careful to speak clearly; yet it all counts for nothing. The person who understands that language hears the same sounds as you do, but those sounds are suffused with meaning. You touched the body of that language; the other person touched body and soul. In some such way the soul suffuses the body; it is the meaning of the body. It is not a 'thing' lurking inside it. It is its meaning, its *logos*, its radiance. It is its life – and how could the life of something be separate from the thing itself? Bluntly put: your soul is the difference between you and your dead body.

When your soul 'departs' at death, it is not as if one part of you has left and the other remains behind. You have disappeared completely; what is left behind is not you. We know this by instinct. In a remote part of Ireland a simple man died. A neighbour, feeling as awkward as the family itself at being the focus of attention, said to the priest during the funeral, 'Excuse me, Father, the corpse's brother would like a word with you.' Why do we find this a very odd expression? Because we know that corpses don't have brothers. Corpses don't have anything. What is most striking about the appearance of a dead body is the total absence of involvement with us at every level. Our attentions, our tears, our feelings of desolation are unable to bring the person back. We tiptoe around the room as if he or she were only sick; we can't believe just yet in the total absence; that is something we will have to grow into gradually. The departure of a 'soul' is the departure of a whole person, even though alive you were fully body and fully soul.

'The body is more in the soul than the soul is in the body,' said Eckhart. This probably doesn't mean anything very clear, but at least it helps to shake up our categories and loosen their overbearing authority. Think of the body, then, as a live coal in the fire which is the soul. If it is taken out of the fire and put to the side it soon becomes a cold dead thing, it has nothing to do with fire and heat any more. The dead body is not the person you knew; it is only a mound of chemicals and minerals; the person has disappeared completely.

Where? Where is your friend now? Where are your father and mother? Is there any forwarding address? The only forwarding address of a dead person is God; we cannot reach that person any more except in God; we cannot touch them without touching God. Death is the realisation of God's promise to be 'all in all.'

But how, or even what, is your friend now? Death obviously makes a big difference to a person. What is a bodiless human soul? Not anything that we can really call a person, St Thomas Aquinas said. Christian teaching leaves us with the affirmation that the dead know God, but does not attempt to say anything further. Which may be just as well. We are already only too eager to imagine a bodiless existence. It is better to leave the matter unclear and indistinct. We don't need to be able to figure everything out; 'ask no more than what Christ has provided for your journey through life,' wrote Clement at the end of the first century. 'What we are to be in the future has not been revealed,' wrote John around the same time (1 John 3:2). Rather than try to imagine what a bodiless existence might be like in the next life, we might try and live an egoless existence now: that is our homework. And it will give us a better basis for imagining the kind of existence that the dead might have.

Along with the idea of the soul as a thing we have the idea of heaven, hell and purgatory as places – and so the mystery of human destiny begins to look like sorting things in boxes. In the strange ways we sometimes talk about these 'places', what is missing is any vital reference to God. (What's left if you leave God out?) But we know nothing about heaven except that 'it' is the presence of God, nor about hell than that it is God's absence, nor about purgatory than that it is a process of purification for allowing God to be all in all.

Let's banish that idea of the soul as a sort of slack bubble inside us. In its place let's say 'life', 'my life' – not in the sense of my span of life or my lifetime, but in the sense of that mysterious and yet perfectly ordinary difference between me and my dead body. Let God sort out the psychology of the dead, while we look to what we mean by souls that are still animating bodies. We will find, I believe, that any improvement in the idea we have of the soul is also an improvement in the idea we have of God – and of those ultimate 'places'.

The freshness of it …

When death takes someone who was close to you, it has come close to you; it has brushed your sleeve. Tell yourself, if you will, that it is part of life, as natural as birth, but still it is 'the prince of terrors'. It prevents you from settling down with one set of ideas about life – and especially about death. It pulls you up by the very roots. To tell the truth, we don't know what it is like to die; we only know what it is like for us when one of our family or a friend dies. Their life is changed utterly, but we don't know what it is like for them, nor what it will be like for us.

The trouble with accounts of 'near death experiences' is that none of those people actually died; they experienced some vivid dream at the extremity of life, but they did not cross over into death. We are still in the dark about the reality of death itself. It will be a new experience when we enter it ourselves, not a practised run. When a friend is dying, we are left on the outside, unable to offer our rude health, our strength, to pull them through. (How we would want to!) We look at cats and dogs and we want to shout, 'What right have they to be alive when my father lies dead – or my friend?' But we can do nothing, death makes strangers of us, we are helpless to help them. It is truly the prince of terrors.

There were once two friends, one of whom played the flute while the other listened. Then one day the listener died. The flute player broke his flute and never played again. When people who are close to you die they take part of you with them into death. Who will listen to your stories now? Who will praise your work? Their own life is utterly changed and they have changed yours utterly. There is a terrible finality about it. For all the ages to come, your parents or your friends will never walk the earth again, their faces will never be seen, their voices never heard. But doesn't this give a sharpness to everything? How would it be if the background were an endless sameness, like mirrors reflecting each other to infinity? Instead there is a poignancy, a once-for-all quality about everything in our life. Our life is a unique gift from God; it never existed before and will never be repeated for all eternity. We had better take a good look at everyone, because in a while they will be dead and they will never come this way again.

The ego, which is a fictitious self, would like to perpetuate itself into an eternity of sameness: the same longing and regretting, lusting and taking revenge, sweating and cheating and feeling sorry for itself. Why? Because it doesn't know how to give itself away. We have this craving for immortality and we make it sound really impressive and profound. But, as someone said, many long for immortality who don't know what to do with themselves on a rainy Sunday afternoon. Does the Gospel promise us that our fictitious self, our ego, will live forever? No, thank God.

The ego does not inherit the promise of the resurrection. What we hope to see raised up with Christ is a self that is certainly ours but which we seldom glimpse and which we may have spent most of our lives avoiding. That is our being, our genuine self. It carries the wounds of a lifetime, it is drastically limited; but it knows how to give itself away, how to love, how to worship.... Since it knows how to give itself away it doesn't crave to live forever.

So this is how it stands, you say: the you that would like to survive won't, and the you that may survive doesn't care whether it survives or not! So there's no problem!

All right. It is a bit too schematic, but it is far better than congregations of egos begging God to let them live forever.

Yes, we will go into eternity very naked indeed; we will have been pulled up by the roots. But imagine the freshness of what might happen then!

... *and the depth*

I have a young friend whose whole world is boyfriends, clothes and aerobics. She is also terrified of death, more than most. I am aware that in befriending me she is also probably coming as close to thinking about death as she is able at the moment: I have a grey beard! One day she will speak seriously to me about death; at present she can only speak of it by allusion. Like the grim reaper himself I am watching and waiting! I know death by proxy and I am not so afraid, or at least I think I am not, at the moment. I want to speak of it, not in order to draw this child from her pleasures, but to bring death into the human circle. It surrounds our life on every side; how could we pretend that it is not there? It is part of the equation; how could we enter our humanity deeply without reflecting on it?

The knowledge of death gives you depth, whether you like it or not. It forces you to see the shape of your life, since you have to imagine it finished. If you are in a cloud you cannot see the cloud's shape, so you have the impression that it has no limits; these can be seen only from the outside. You have to imagine your life finished some day, so you cannot avoid thinking of its shape. How does it look when you think of it like this? It looks particular, limited, local; it is such-and-such, it is not the limitless thing you imagined. There will be a time when no further avoidance of realities, no further postponement of depth, will be possible.

Every moment of our life is profound because in a sense it is the last; it is the first and last time this moment is happening. (I wonder if the fascination that many western people have with reincarnation is only a disguised fear of death?) The moment is profound only if you know how to let it pass, how not to be greedy. Why are we not taught a science of living the moment fully and then letting it pass? It would be the most important of all sciences. You try to hold onto the moment because you have not lived it and therefore you want to keep it for later. But when you think of death you know that postponement comes to an end. So death teaches you how to live with depth.

I have found that the times and places where I poured out my life were precisely the times and places that I left most easily. I trust that this experience, if I enter it deeply, will teach me in the end how to leave all time and place, how to leave this sweet life.

The ego's heaven

Only our true self can face death and the thought of death; the ego cannot. We may never have lived from our true self since early childhood, or we may have had only brief glimpses of it. It is a deeper resource than we know. It sometimes astounds us, especially when we are in an emergency and we do not have time to think and align things with our ego. Have you ever felt that there was much more to you than you knew? If we could live always from that source we would know how to face death and the thought of death.

When the ego tries to face the thought of death it invents a facile 'beyond', a delectable heaven that is only a continuation of egocentric desire; effectively it denies death. The ego would like above all to survive (in the comfort to which it is accustomed). See the beefy guy with the fat cigar and the greedy eyes.... No, I am not referring to any individual; he is a symbol of the ego. He would not like to die, he would like to live forever, doing even better for himself in eternity than his gluttonous imagination can hope for. The ego's heaven would be hell for everyone else, a lurid projection of cupidity.

Death is the end of time. What is time? In practice it is oneself. When you give an hour of your time to someone, you are giving an hour of yourself. Now while the ego can give away some of its time, for this or that purpose, it cannot give it all away – any more than you can pull yourself up by your own bootstraps. In fact it craves more and more time, that is, more and more of itself. Death is when all one's time is given or taken away. The ego cannot face death. This is why its heaven is a false one: there has been no transition, no change, no passage; it is a wish to continue as before, to survive.

Christian teaching offers us no hope of survival; there is nothing in it for the ego. It proclaims something quite different: the hope of resurrection from the dead. We will go through every inch of death; we will be spared nothing. Not only the body but the ego will die utterly. We don't take death seriously enough; there have been too many superficial denials of its reality, too many euphemisms. Part of the unreality is that we don't take Christ's death seriously. We can easily have the most superficial idea of his resurrection as a kind of conjuring trick: that he played dead for a couple of days, only to come back to show us that there's light around the corner and that death isn't real at all. This is in keeping with many of the things we believe superficially about Jesus: principally that he wasn't fully human in the first place. The Church's teaching is that he was 'fully human and fully divine.' But many take this to mean that he was half human and half divine. No, he was fully human, and therefore he experienced death to the full.

God raised him from death, not from a simulation of death. (The New Testament does not say that he raised himself from the dead, but that 'God raised him.') It is on this that our hope of resurrection is based, and on nothing else. Philosophical 'proofs' of the soul's immortality are only a forlorn expression of longing or wishful thinking. Death is a real passage and there is no survival, no immortality; but our faith offers us the hope of resurrection.

What will be raised up in the resurrection? The ego? No, the ego will die an eternal death; it never was more than a pretence in the first place. What is in us from God will be raised up, the real self that God made and that I am so infrequently in touch with. Our faith tells us to forsake the ego now, before we have to anyway, and to live lives that look towards God. It tells us to let go of egocentric desire, to live beyond the self-centred self – in the language of the Gospel, 'to lay down our life'. Lay down your life, it tells us, before it is taken from you anyway; get used to living from the self that God made in you; then you may live in the hope of resurrection. But (one parting question), what is it like to hope for something that is not egocentric?

The weaver's shuttle

My first thought was that they were dead! Thousands had died here recently in the eruption of Mount Pinatubo. My head was full of stories of tragedy: villages engulfed and people buried alive in the grey ash they call *lahar*, houses collapsing, a friend of mine narrowly escaping death. There were bodies lying every-where. But in a moment I realised that these were all lying on mattresses strewn on the ground! It was siesta time in a small textile factory. This northern part of the Philippines is famous for weaving. In the hottest hour of the day it is impossible to work, so those girls just pull out mattresses and lie down to sleep in the workplace. None woke up as we arrived: work had taken half their energy and the heat had taken the rest. I was for leaving; I felt we had intruded into a bedroom; but the others, all Filipinos, insisted on showing me everything: the work, the looms, the fabrics. In hot countries the distinction between inside and outside, private and public, is not so clearly marked, and sometimes not at all. We stepped most carefully over the beautiful reclining forms and examined their morning's work.

The looms lay silent and still, resting, like the young women who had been working them. The shuttles that shoot from side to side, almost faster than the eye can see, were stopped dead. They were like lifeless birds. 'My days are swifter than a weaver's shuttle,' cried Job, in a sudden moment of knowing life's piteous fragility and transience. Here the silence, the memories of Mount Pinatubo, the bodies lying about in a semblance of death, our own whispers, and remembering Job: everything conspired to create a raw awareness in the mind. Then came the memory of other ages and places: Pompeii, near Naples, over-whelmed, along with other cities, by the eruption of Mount Vesuvius, on the 24th of August, 79 A.D. All life was stopped and fixed forever under sixty feet of pumice stone fragments and volcanic ash. Modern excavators found public buildings, houses, shops, with all their detail (a shop still had the name clearly legible over the door; in one of the houses there was a cake in the oven). As they excavated they frequently found cavities, which they filled with plaster, later removing the surrounds to reveal perfect replicas of people who were engulfed as they attempted to escape. The contortions of their fallen bodies, the folds of their clothes ... all were captured in poignant detail, as life froze suddenly on that morning, nineteen centuries ago.... Mount Vesuvius in Italy, Mount Pinatubo in the Philippines, the prostrate bodies in the textile factory, the silence.... I had to leave quickly, so vivid was the sensation of calamity.

Human beings are vulnerable, they are quite easily destroyed. The tender grass is trodden underfoot, or it grows rank and dies; but there is always a tenderness that remains in human beings, no matter how rank they may appear. It is the knowledge of death that keeps us tender, that terrible knowledge that other living beings do not have to bear. It is no virtue, I am sure, to be morbid about death, always 'to see the skull beneath the skin.' But surely this hard knowledge, this truth, must be able to do something beautiful and profound for us. The truth, Jesus said, will set you free. The truth of death feels sad, yes, but sadness has a quality of depth about it; if we were forever content we would be like cattle or sheep. The knowledge of death prevents us from becoming hard and fully identified with this or that. Of course if we deny this knowledge we become harder still: there is a kind of heartlessness in people who are on the run from it. But when we live with it, it makes us more human, softer, more tolerant. All our lives we have been thinking about Jesus's death and seeing representations of it, and associating this with self-giving, with wisdom deeper than the wisdom of the Greeks, with forgiveness, with heroic love. Even apart from the power of his Passion, this is an incredibly profound education; it has gone into our bloodstream and our bones. It must be almost impossible for a Christian to die like a pagan.

We are like the grass of the field, says the psalm. But the

intention was not to make light of our life and death, for it is surely heartbreaking to see people die, and to know that 'in the midst of life we are in death.' There is an unbearable sadness about prostrate bodies. In the physical presence of death we have little to say, and this is just as well. Job, too, was almost reduced to silence:

> I spoke once, but I have no answer –
> twice, but I will say no more (40:5).

It was enough; he had already spoken his immortal words, which Christians throughout the ages have made their own:

> I know that my Redeemer lives,
> and that in the end he will stand upon the earth (19:25).

'87'

This prison had no gates. It didn't need them. You could call it an open prison. Nor was it even a building in the proper sense. 'Where's the catch?' I hear you saying. The catch is that it was dug out of solid rock, and the opening was at the top, twenty feet above the reach of the tallest man. Through that narrow hole the prisoner was lowered by a rope into the dark and squalid interior. If the very thought of it is terrible, and the sight of it makes your flesh creep, there can be no words to describe the experience of being imprisoned there.

Today you can enter the prison by a staircase. But why, you ask, would anyone want to go there? Why, because it was the prison where Jesus was held the night before his execution.

Inside that dark pit today (there are lights now) you can read on the wall the words of Psalm 87. Never was a psalm more appropriate to a place. Jesus, who certainly knew all the psalms by heart, must have prayed that psalm over and over on that terrible night. Earlier in the evening all his friends had fled, and in the courtyard just above, Peter had denied all knowledge of him. He was alone in the dark and condemned to crucifixion.

Lord my God, I call for help by day,
I cry at night before you ...
For my soul is filled with evils,
my life is on the brink of the grave,
I am reckoned as one in the tomb,
I have reached the end of my strength,
like one alone among the dead,
like the slain lying in their graves,
like those you remember no more
cut off as they are from your hand.
You have laid me in the depths of the tomb,
in places that are dark, in the depths ...
You have taken away my friends
and made me hateful in their sight.
Imprisoned, I cannot escape,
my eyes are sunken with grief....
To you I stretch out my hands....
Lord, why do you reject me?
Why do you hide your face ... ?
Friend and neighbour you have taken away:
my one companion is darkness.

To stand there, even today, is to know faith as a necessity. The reality of Jesus's suffering bears down on you with overwhelming force. As your body cannot escape through those rock walls, neither can your mind evade the reality of what lies before you. It is a sobering thing to be put in prison, even for ten minutes, with the truth.

But there is now a stairs, as I said. When you come up from there, you know that you can never again play the sophisticate, you cannot have a shallow and superior attitude to the faith and to believers. The faith has deep roots underground; Jesus's human spirit agonised there during an interminable night. When you emerge you also know something else, equally compelling: that you can never again be indifferent to the countless ways in which human beings are imprisoned by hatred, ignorance and addiction, by a shallow popular culture (bred on capitalism) that has no love for anything, by exploitation of every kind, by illness, broken relationships and betrayal....

Every Friday night, the Prayer of the Church includes this Psalm 87. It is prayed not only by priests and religious but by an increasing number of lay people. Through all these the Church carries again in its heart the memory of the Lord's imprisonment, and the imprisonment of all his brothers and sisters throughout the ages and throughout the earth.

Gethsemane

She was a deep quiet woman, a Zulu, and we often asked her to speak and sing in her own language, so that we could listen again with amazement to the distinctive 'clicks'. We must have seemed strange to her, because to her those clicks were not at all strange; they were just consonants like any other, and it was like being asked by strangers to say words with the letter 't' or 'p' in them.

She was taking part in a renewal course, which was to end with a pilgrimage to the Holy Land. Two weeks before the end, she got word that her father had died. In her culture it is unthinkable to miss a parent's funeral. But it was impossible for her now to arrive on time. After much agonising she decided to come with us to the Holy Land and to pray there for her father. Then on the day before our departure she received news that her mother also had just died. The problem with flights was just as before: she could not possibly arrive on time for the funeral. Torn by grief and remorse she came with us to Tel Aviv and then by bus to Jerusalem. We celebrated the first Mass of the pilgrimage that evening in the Garden of Gethsemane. It was the very day of her mother's funeral, and when we calculated the time difference we found to our astonishment that it was also the very hour.

'My soul is overwhelmed with sorrow to the point of death. Stay here and keep watch with me.' Gethsemane is the very word for sorrow throughout the ages; this small garden is as wide as the world. It is also called the Garden of Olives, and there are ancient olive trees growing everywhere around. The olive tree is indestructible, they say: even if you cut it to the ground again and again it will grow again from the root; it can live for thousands of years. So they tell us, at any rate. If there is any truth in it, some of these may have been silent witnesses to the Lord's agony; some of them may have been there when he said to Peter, James and John, 'Sit here while I go over there and pray.'

A small garden as wide as the world; sorrow as deep as existence itself.... Pleasure and happiness can be very superficial, and being superficial they can be radically private – though their appearance is the very opposite. But sorrow, accepted, opens the heart deeply and enables us to touch the humanity of the whole world. A small garden in the dark of night, four countrymen in the city, hanging around doing nothing: a passer-by would see nothing whatsoever. But some weeks later the whole world would see. 'Parthians, Medes, Elamites; residents of Mesopotamia, Judea and Cappadocia, Pontus and Asia, Phrygia and Pamphylia, Egypt and the part of Libya near Cyrene; visitors from Rome ... Cretans and Arabs ...' (Acts 2:10-11). And Zulus.

The sorrow of death, the universal sorrow. We had come from the corners of the earth to Gethsemane, bringing with us the knowledge of death and the hope of seeing its meaning. It is not only universal but the oldest of all sorrows, and the newest when it comes near us. All times and places curve into that small garden across the valley of Kedron.

The newest sorrow when it touches us.... Our moments of sorrow, said Rilke, 'are the moments when something new has entered into us, something unknown; our feelings grow mute in shy perplexity, everything in us withdraws, a stillness comes, and the new, which no one knows, stands in the midst of it and is silent.'

A stillness comes, he said. 'Sleep now and take your rest,' said Jesus to the drowsy disciples. The agonising moment of decision had passed, he was at peace. History had been divided in two by that moment; the new reality, which no one knows, stood before their eyes, and they turned over and went to sleep. The new and the old are together in us. He understood: 'Sleep now ... ' he said. When their time came they would understand; it would be soon enough. Peter and James died martyrs' deaths, John died in advanced old age. They came through that terrible garden, but their word was the joy of eternal life, not the sorrow of death. 'The life appeared; we have seen it and testify to it; and we proclaim to you that eternal life, which was with the Father and has appeared to us' (1 John 1).

TWO

Leave-taking

Past and future faces

I gave lumps of clay to a group of people and asked them to make an image of their past and future. There should not be two images, I suggested, because the past and future, though distinct, are connected with each other. Nor should there be only one image, because past and future are not one: they are not one and they are not two. This was a difficult task, but there is no use in asking people to do easy things: if something is easy, people are likely do it quickly and with little attention; but if it is difficult they have to think and be alert, they have to make a mental journey.

Potter's clay is like the stuff that dreams are made of. When you handle a lump of clay, the inconstant shapes suggest different things, and one thing changes effortlessly into another – just as in the world of dreams. Clay is a good substance for dreaming with. As in the world of dreams all kinds of impossible things become possible: something can even be one and two at the same time.

One woman, a philosophy lecturer, made a boat. In itself a boat is a fairly obvious image of the journey through life. This boat was about six inches long, but the unexpected element for her was the prow: it developed into a large human head, not looking proudly forward as prows do, but back into the boat. A corresponding head sprouted from the stern, and these two stood facing each other along the length of the boat. They were her past and future, she said. And yes, she emphasised, they were not one and they were not two.

'She's a professor, you see,' her friend explained.

She had not planned anything, her boat had just happened.

But looking at it now she saw extraordinary significance in it. Bending over her creation she began to talk about it. As you go forward in your life, she said, your past and future are always staring each other in the face. One face looks back continually: it is so preoccupied with the past that it *is* the past, it is what happened before. But that is the face that enters the future first, though backwards of course. In a certain sense your past precedes you into the future. You have made yourself a certain kind of person, up to this moment; you have built up habits and preferences that shaped you. Your past, in practice, has a certain momentum, even though, theoretically, you could act out of character at any time. 'When I say *you* I mean *we*, of course,' she said; 'I even mean Rosemary!' she added, teasing her friend.

Then the other head: as you look and move into the future you are continually looking into the face and over the shoulder of the past. The past is always part of your horizon, even if you choose to ignore it. It is always looking straight at you, even when you turn your boat to left or right. For this very reason it is all too easy to identify yourself with it: it is the face that is ever before you. But the future is a face you cannot see; it is too close to you. It is the face you are shaping this instant.

'Mary,' said her friend to her, 'you're talking like poured concrete!'

But the professor continued. Professors always do. Apart from that face that ever looks at you from the past, she said, your life is an open horizon. No wonder you identify so fiercely with that face of the past! It is your evidence that you are something in particular and not nothing. So you cling to it as to life itself. But that is a drowning man's grip: a clinging to death, not to life. Panic makes you cling to what you have been. I see this quite often in myself, she said. Much of what we call tradition is this panic in the face of the unknown.

'May we take a break now?' said her friend, who had no taste for heavy considerations.

'Later!' she replied, and continued once again (she must be one of those professors who go on lecturing after the bell).

Clinging to death, she said, we claim to love life. It may mean that we feel protected for the moment, that we are reassured by that face that goes before us, the face of the past pretending to be the future. We should try to break its mesmerising stare, try to be free, try to take leave of it....

'Yes, but how?' said someone else.

'I don't know ... I don't know.'

But her friend was right too. Let's not forget to take a break and to breathe anyway. There was one who understood us from the beginning. His disciples were crossing the lake when a storm blew up and the frail boat was in danger of sinking. 'Help us!' they shouted at the One who lay sleeping in the stern. 'Why are you so filled with fear?' he asked. 'Where is your faith?'

Transience

> The beauty of the world has made me sad,
> This beauty that will pass. (P.H. Pearse)

May I ask a question out of order: what would the world be like if nothing ever passed away? There would never be anything new. Everything would be old but unable to die. It would be like Sartre's world in *Nausea:* just *there*, meaningless, mouldering, superfluous. We are mercifully spared that. There is plenty of change and excitement in the world: enough to take our breath away, enough to keep us alert and on our feet for a whole lifetime (except, ahem! at the end). Everything around us and in us is transient. If that makes us sad, we should think of what the alternative would do to us!

Still, everyone understands this sadness. It is perhaps a symbol of our own passing. It is good to connect these two, the transience of things and our own transience: they receive a certain resonance from each other. 'Just as in death we must leave each other altogether,' wrote Rilke, 'so at every moment we must give each other up and let each other go and not hold each other back.' He advises us to get into the spirit of transience. We might as well, for how could anyone defeat it? It seems wise to embrace the thing you cannot defeat; wiser still when even wanting to defeat it would be the greatest madness. Swimming, I believe, could teach us much: to swim we have to accept the nature of water, its fluidity, its different reliability from that of firm ground; and we have to avoid putting a drowning man's grip on our friends. Moreover, they tell us that about ninety percent of the human body is water, so it should not be impossible for us to learn fluidity and transience!

Everything passes and it is right that it should pass; that is clear when we think about it. The most transient things of all, one would think, are ideas. But it is not so: we sometimes cling to ideas as to life itself, ideas of who we are and what we want, what is worthwhile and what is worthless, what is possible and what is impossible.... We would get away with this rigidity forever if it were not for death. The thought of death goes deeper than all these other thoughts, and digs them all up. There before us in a moment lies the upturned sod, black and bare, the earthworms recoiling, their poor privacy discovered. It seems a cruel invasion. 'The human being is a being-unto-death,' said Heidegger, but it was not at all his purpose to depress us. He meant that death prevents us from settling down forever with a stunted understanding of ourselves and the world; it thrusts greatness on us, sooner or later. It digs deepest, it is an awesome sowing and reaping.

What freedom it promises, if you don't recoil at the thought of it! It tells you that there is no need to keep anything back, that it is pointless to try. Embrace the inevitable, it says. Leap on the great wave of transience and praise the God of the ages! Why crouch there shivering, unable to decide to plunge? Give everything away, like a diver. The water will teach you. The water of transience.

Every night of life the Church prays in the words of Jesus, 'Into your hands, Lord, I commit my spirit.' In Paschal time it adds, 'Alleluia! Alleluia!'

Pleasure

The English philosopher Thomas Hobbes described life in the state of nature as 'solitary, poor, nasty, brutish and short.' This has often been quoted mistakenly as a reference to life in the Middle Ages. Many people belittle those past centuries in order to say that all enlightenment is a recent thing. But there is wisdom for us in the centuries that have gone before us, if we know how to take leave of them properly.

The 'right to the pursuit of happiness' was built into the American Declaration of Independence at the beginning. It proved to be a headline for a new age. But it is worth our while to ask (not now in reference to the founding documents of any country, but in reference to ourselves), what kind of happiness you achieve when you pursue happiness. What kind of pleasure do you have when you have sought pleasure? There is a self-defeating mechanism built into it.

Pleasure, St Thomas Aquinas wrote in the thirteenth century, is good and not evil; it accompanies the healthy functioning of every human faculty. There is no Puritanism in this; that was for a later age. Johann Tauler wrote in the fourteenth century: 'Pleasures should come and go with the actions that occasion them, but then they should not remain with you.' This sounds like very good sense. There is nothing here about the pursuit of pleasure: in itself a very nervous notion, as well as exhausting, and profoundly cheerless. These people from an older time tell us: do something that is valuable in itself, and pleasure will accompany the doing of it. Happiness and pleasure are side-products: they arise spontaneously when you are doing something else.

Pleasures 'should not remain with you.' What did Tauler mean by this? Look at it this way: when something is over, it is over; to bring it back is to bring back a dead thing, and it is to be dead oneself: not available to what is happening in the present. When we try to prolong some pleasure or bring back an old one, we open the door to addiction, and then follows the self-defeating cycle of pursuit, dissatisfaction, and further pursuit. In this way, if we go to the extreme, we are capable of side-tracking our whole life. Let bygones be bygones, we say, in relation to personal hurts; but it seems we should say it also in relation to pleasures. Let them pass, let me not be attached to them; attachment spoils everything. There are perfect moments that can only happen, that cannot be planned and that cannot be prolonged. In fact the words 'happen' and 'happiness' come from the same root, 'hap' (which is repeated in words like 'perhaps', 'haphazard' and 'hapless'). Happiness has to happen. It is impossible to force these moments in any way. A spontaneous gesture of affection from a friend, or a compliment, or a spirited conversation: when these are planned they become flat and empty. Even in nature there are moments like that: the quality of light falling across a hillside, the behaviour of an animal or bird, a particular hush of wind in the trees. These are moments of natural 'grace', and when Christians speak of divine grace they mean something like that but beyond it. The word 'grace' means 'gift'. Such moments are gifts, gifts of the moment, and they cannot be captured in greedy hands. Many thanks for the wisdom of an older world.

'You are too attached ... to be able to understand what is going on,' Tauler said. It was a throw-away remark, but a statement of deep understanding. Attachment to pleasure blinds us: not to every aspect of a situation, but to every aspect but one. To live a deeply human life requires a great deal of natural intelligence. This intelligence has nothing to do with school or college, and its one subject is life itself. If we become weak in that subject, it matters little how strong we are in any other. The real wisdom, said Tauler, is to be able to respond in the moment to 'whatever God gives, whatever God takes away.'

On becoming human

I knew a man who would defend fanatically everything he had ever identified with in any way, while all the rest he regarded as rubbish. It did not matter at all that this identification was often purely accidental, or very superficial or only imagined; once he put his ego into something, no external force could separate them. If, for example, he had visited a place where no one else in the company had been, that became the only place in the world worth visiting; if he read a book, that alone promoted it to a classic; if he had shaken some politician's hand, that politician became the saviour of the nation. That is the nature of the ego – which means the false self: not my reality, but my idea of what I am, my self-image. Being nothing in itself, it is forever creating images and fictions of itself, living outside itself because it belongs nowhere, wandering in rags but imagining grandeur, like a demented beggar.

Who are you, Ego? Who are you, poor lunatic? Why is every word you speak a lie? Are you something? Are you nothing? Where did you arise? And what great shame sent you out alone to beg along the roads? I am the child of fear so deep that it fled even the knowledge of itself. I am Golem, of Jewish folklore, the quasi-human creature constructed by human beings in imitation of the Creator's work. I was Adam, on whose forehead once stood the Hebrew word *emeth*, 'truth'; but the first letter I erased, and I am become *meth*, 'dead'; I fall to dust. Falling to dust I see nothing but dust; and even God is dust to me.

Can you ever be Adam again? How will you stand in the truth? Yours is a hardhearted poverty, there is no compassion in it. It is not truly poverty but cupidity: an unrelenting possessiveness. You must become Adam with his soft flesh, *yarek* – the very word means 'to be soft'. Stand naked there, trembling, new-made, Adam, poor child of the dust of earth. Tremble, but do not run to hide yourself, do not make fictions to cover your nakedness. Your glory is *emeth*, truth, shining vulnerably in your eyes; it is not possessed, but shining. How could you possess the truth? No more than you can possess the sun or the stars. It is around you, within you, everywhere, shining. Shining darkly, strangely, everlasting.

Turn back from fictions to the place where fictions arise. See them in their genesis; see how you created a false heaven and a false earth. See how you divided the waters above from the waters below: precious and mean, mine and yours, 'one of us' and 'not one of us'. See the false lights of your firmament, a mock sun and tinsel stars: your guiding thoughts. See the trail of death behind you, a poisoned world, its creatures dying. See all that you have made. And see Golem, the self-made man, Ego, with his tormented brain. Then turn away from all this, from your false heaven and earth, from your fictions, from your impressive thoughts, your preferences, your selective principles; or rather turn them away: they have no existence. Seeing their unreality you will be free of them.

Enter deeply into that freedom; know it, not as an idea but as a place, yet limitless. From that place, everything becomes strangely actual. For an instant know the feel of absolute silence, with no striving of the mind or will. That is a real place in you, it is not another fiction. When you look out from there you are Adam and not Golem, a child of God and not a jaded false god. You see the world full of beings at once splendid and transient. You want to open your heart to them, to meet them directly, to be one with them....

That sad egocentric man I mentioned, died. He died as he had lived, considering also his death superior to other deaths. For years he had controlled people by means of his sickness. From his deathbed, for months, he tyrannised his family, enslaving them to his wishes. Right to the end, the light in his eyes was cupidity. Then one evening the light faded and he went the way of all flesh. But between the death of his ego and the death of his body, in that moment – who knows? – Adam was born, and the new Adam, Christ: born and died in the same moment, in the same moment died and perhaps came to life.

On becoming tired of yourself

Your name please? Write it here _____ . Now repeat after me, if you like: 'I am fed up with _____ , and I would like to be rid of him/her.' No, of course I am not suggesting suicide, nor even self-hatred. I am suggesting that you get away from yourself (of course when I say you I mean me too: we). 'You need to get away for a while,' people often advise you. But the trouble is that you bring yourself with you: all your old ideas, your habits, addictions and prejudices, your fears, your careful inclusions and exclusions ... just the same as always. How can we stand it? We try and cope by getting drunk now and then, or by becoming infatuated with someone, or by over-sleeping or becoming a 'couch-potato'. All of these have the deepest spiritual significance: they are substitutes for renunciation.

Now let's hear the other side. Surely we have to be nicer to ourselves than that! It is as natural to maintain one's personality as it is to maintain the body. Every person is something particular and limited, and we should not hate ourselves for being finite! God loves us just as we are; we are beautiful in God's sight, even if not in our own. To go rejecting oneself as you propose is to try and have better taste than God.

Now the first side again. A human being is not a little solid ball, just itself, occupying its own space, excluding everything else. We are open by our very nature. To diminish that openness is unnatural. Aristotle said, 'The human soul is, in a way, everything.' But because of modern commercialism (and all that goes with it) we tend to see ourselves in competition with everyone else: you and I, or rather your ego and mine, compete for space; we can negotiate to our mutual advantage, but we cannot really share anything – billiard balls don't.

The Christian spirit stands directly against this. The first disciples held all things in common: 'All who believed were together and had all things in common' (Acts 2:44). How do you share something with others? By taking leave of yourself, I think, by getting tired of yourself.

Yes, we are beautiful, but the ego is always unlovely, poor thing! It is not God's creation, but our own. It is very visible in uncultivated persons, such as children or shamelessly selfish adults; but it is worse when it is hidden behind a veneer of culture. It cannot be improved, it can only be abandoned.

How?

That is at once a very long and a very short story. The short story is that it is possible, in a moment of utter stillness, to step out of the ego. The long story is how we are to live in order to make this possible. We have to study the workings of the ego with great attention, even respect, and then live clear of them, as far as we are able. For instance, we can choose constantly, in one situation after another, to do the generous thing without calling it the virtue of generosity. And we can choose not to follow the counsels of fear. The ego tells you, 'Be prudent (read 'selfish'), be careful ('calculate your own interests'), be sensible ('imagine what people will think').' In other words, turn back. But instead of turning back (this is how I put it to myself) bring your chest up against the difficulty, gently, and keep going. What can you do to get away from yourself? Bring your chest up against the next thing you have to do, gently, and keep going. Don't run away, and don't come in with your fists up. Instead, bring your chest gently forward. It is the place where your heart is. It is also the strength of your presence. You are undefended, but for that very reason you can withstand everything. Don't consider the dangers first, or the benefits to your ego: if you do, you have already turned back.

How imprudent!

But it is far more imprudent to reinforce your habit of turning back. At the end of our lives we may want to congratulate ourselves on all the trouble we have avoided, but I have never heard that sentiment from the lips of a dying person.

When you try to live in this unselfish way you are being very good, are you not?

That is another trap, perhaps the most treacherous of all. There is something grotesque about 'practising virtues'; it is the work of a certain type of ego, and it is no better than any other. See how subtly the ego always slips back into place. This is the meaning of that 'difficult verse' in the Gospel, 'When you have done all that is commanded you, say, "We are unprofitable

servants; we have only done what was our duty" ' (Luke 17:10).
Become tired of yourself, he seems to say, and give yourself up
like a bad habit!

Toby

A friend still remembers me leaning out of the window at 1 a.m.,
shouting at the dog, 'Toby, shut up! Shut up, man!' How do you
teach a dog to stop barking? I didn't teach Toby that night, nor
any night. But he taught me something of lasting value. He
taught me how to cope with noise. (And by extension, with
anything that I don't like. But I'll come to that.)

The first lesson in coping with noise is: listen to it. This may
sound too elementary, but Toby was new to teaching at the time.
Most people try not to listen, but this never works; the more you
try not to listen, the better you listen and the wider awake you
become. Instead, listen! Dogs, we can presume, always have
proportionate reasons for barking, though these reasons may
not appear proportionate to us. Barking is likely to be hard work,
particularly when prolonged, and dogs have the name of being
lazy; they would not do it if they did not consider it urgently
necessary. Let them bark, they are attending to the world for you
while you lie in bed. It is not the barking that is keeping you
awake, but your resistance to it. Stop resisting and listen.

Anything that you exclude becomes your enemy and comes
back to break down your door. But anything that you include
can sit down in peace with you and be your friend.

'But ... but ... !'

Yes, I know. There are things we should not allow in: there
are destructive ways of thinking, there are corrosive desires and
vicious fantasies. You cannot sit down in peace with these, you
have to try and keep your inner being clean. But now, compare
all those vicious things with poor blameless Toby! He never yet
betrayed a friend, nor bit the hand that fed him, never claimed
unmerited promotion nor was ambitious for anything more
than to be taken for a walk. Years ago he formed an unquestion-

ing alliance with you, not based on your merits but on his own trustful nature, and he overlooks insults such as 'Shut up, man!' Know your enemies: Toby and his kind are not among them. Meditate on his innocence, listen to his voice, include him in your life, tell him in your mind that he has your permission to continue, that he may bark till morning, but that you will not be able to appreciate his voice all that time, for you need to sleep … to sleep.…

Toby's teaching career is only beginning. If you have learnt your first lesson well and become an expert in coping with noise, you can go on to higher studies. In place of noise take some persons whom you don't naturally like. As you listen to their voices, transpose them to Toby's voice; as you look into their eyes, remember Toby's innocence; as they continue to talk, give them permission and even encouragement by the very quality of your presence to them. You are not trapped, you are free at every moment to take your leave; but while you are present do not exclude them; consciously include them in your life. We have all compromised ourselves in a thousand ways, we are frail human beings, we all deserve another chance. Give those persons a new chance, don't be the person you have always been with them: be a new person; it will do you and them a world of good. Give every dog his day … !

Suppose your dislike is for some job you have to do, whether occasionally or every day. You have Toby and his kind, the best of teachers; you know how to go about it. Don't begin by condemning and resisting. Begin by being receptive. Look and listen and be patient; don't run ahead in a rut; have a fresh mind, be a new person; take it slowly and without prejudice. Open your eyes and see something new in it, something you never paid any attention to before. Include this job in your life, don't exclude it. (You cannot exclude it anyway, because it is something you have to do.)

It is very paradoxical: the only way to be free of something is to embrace it fully; if you push it away it will follow you forever. Leave-taking is subtle rather than difficult. I have found the most wearisome jobs transformed in this way. I have learnt things I would never have learnt by any other means. I have found great peace. And I find that I can do more work and get less tired.

It's easy for me. I had the best of teachers.

Nostalgia

I met a young Ethiopian woman whose name was Mitike, which means 'Replacement'. Her sister had died at the age of three, and the new baby was named accordingly. I asked her if she liked her name and she replied yes.

Replacement O'Shaughnessy, Replacement Fogarty.... No, it would not work elsewhere. I never met anyone but Mitike who liked to be called Replacement. How would you even shorten it?

What about *being* a replacement? That's different, it would even flatter us sometimes. If you replace an important person, you feel important yourself. But do we ever in fact replace one another? I once said to some people that I replaced so-and-so in this job (a wise old man, greatly loved), and one of them said, 'No, you didn't!' People can be materially replaced, it is true. When you are about to leave a job, people say you are irreplaceable; but on the following Monday a stranger is doing your work. And cemeteries, we are reminded none too gently, are full of irreplaceable people. But – and the pain of this 'but' is the pain of life itself – things are not the same as before. They may be better, but they are not the same. Time has moved on and the world is all different. You miss what has been, and you are not comforted for the loss. That is the very name of nostalgia: looking at present things and people with unseeing eyes and remembering what was before. Everything looks cheap and second-hand, the only reality is in the memory. Your life is a reluctant train journey: you have to move on with the world, a broken-hearted passenger, while everything you care about remains behind.

The passage of time is the saddest of all mysteries. You have only to look back to see for yourself that everything turns to dust. 'Not people die, but worlds die in them,' wrote the Russian poet Yevtushenko. Every day a world dies and a world is born. Equally. But if your eyes are always straining for the past, you will miss what is being born around you. Yevtushenko's own case is instructive. At the age of eight he wrote his first novel. Paper was scarce, so he wrote it between the lines of his grandmother's copy of *Das Kapital!* The human reality creeps in everywhere, most often in a childish hand. And it is full of imagination. Poetry is not just antique words; it is the present too, so young, so fresh that it makes revolutionary tracts look old-fashioned. If the poems you remember from school were the nostalgic lays of the Romantics, you will tend to expect all poetry to be sweetly sad and wistful. But there is stronger drink than that.

You don't have to look far away to see the past: it is falling away just behind your heels. It is here. Look at the present and you will see that it is dying and changing into the past, moment by moment. In place of the sweet sadness of nostalgia you can experience terror! You can know the mystery of time at such close quarters that there is no room left for the self-indulgence of nostalgia. Past and present are the one mystery. Every moment is a leave-taking.

That unpractised hand is yours; we are all new-born to the present. Are you nostalgic still for your childhood? Your real childhood is now, your historical childhood is only a memory. Be alive in this newest part of your life before it floats away. If you cannot do this, I doubt that you could enjoy that historical childhood you long for, were it restored to you. Why do so many older people go about looking so miserable: so burdened, so rigid, so humourless ... ? It is because they have forgotten that they are children. It is no wonder they look like cheerless exiles; they are separated by many decades from their childhood, while they should not be separated from it by even one moment.

But did I not say that every moment is a moment of death? Yes, and it is also a moment of birth; it is birth and death at once, and you can look at it one way or the other.

You can look at it one way or the other, but better than either, no doubt, is to see it as both together. Seeing each moment as a birth, you will stay fresh in mind and heart; seeing it as death you will not greedily try to possess it. Life will come every moment, a fresh gift from God; you will receive it with joy and in the same moment you will let it go, perhaps with sadness, or with terror. There will be joy and sadness together, and terror: the salt taste of life itself.

Where you would rather not go

Long ago when the world was young and many of today's clever things had not yet been thought of, there was a king who had a son to whom he was greatly attached. So solicitous was he that he had the whole palace carpeted with sheepskins, to protect the royal baby feet from the hardness of the floors (shoes had not yet been invented). When he got a little bigger, the child wanted to romp outside, so his father gave orders to carpet the entire grounds of the palace with sheepskins. This meant that many hundreds of sheep had to be slaughtered, but nothing was too much when it came to the little prince's comfort. When the prince was seventeen years old his father arranged to send him on business to another kingdom, and ordered that his path should be carpeted in the usual way. The man in charge of the sheep was distraught at the prospect of so much slaughter, and he went away quietly to think what he could do. Next day he returned, and his eyes were bright with intelligence. He went to the king and said, 'Your Majesty, instead of slaughtering thousands of sheep why don't we kill just one, and cut out two patches of its hide, and attach them to the prince's feet?' The king, being an intelligent man, saw the wisdom of this immediately; and so it was done. And that is how shoes were invented.

Many inventions, as we know, turn out to have a wider application than appeared at first. Generalising the insight that gave rise to the world's first pair of shoes, you could state the following:

- A small change in yourself is equivalent to a big change in reality.
- Unless you change yourself, all the other changes you bring about will be pointless and repetitive.

Alcibiades, a vain young man in ancient Greece, told Socrates that he was off to see the world. 'You will not see it,' said Socrates, 'unless you leave Alcibiades at home.' You will not only be unable to change anything, you will not even be able to see anything clearly unless you change yourself.

But why change? Am I not all right as I am?

Yes! But everything is changing continually, and if you stop you will be in the way! In sober reality you are changing, whether you like it or not; you are getting older every hour; you are on the high seas and the wind is blowing; how could you dream of remaining unchanged? To live is to change, someone said, and to live deeply is to have changed much. You are changing, never fear! The trouble is that you are not changing enough: you are continually defending yourself, and defending everything you ever did, always trying to prove that you are right! You don't need to do that! If you try to change other people (and things) without changing yourself, the results will be disastrous. The greatest damage is done to the world by revolutionaries who want to change everything except themselves. This is the boring thing about revolutions: the wheel does the full circle and the revolutionaries become in turn the oppressors.

> Hurrah for revolution and cannon-shot!
> A beggar on horseback lashes a beggar on foot.
> Hurrah for revolution and cannon come again!
> The beggars have changed places, but the lash goes on.
> (W. B. Yeats)

Change is always ambiguous, never more so than when I try to change myself. The problem is this 'I' that changes according to its own standard. That standard may be high or low, but it is certainly partisan; it is my idea of who I am, and my idea of who

I want to be. When I have changed according to my own idea of change, it is likely that the change is more apparent than real; there still has been no leave-taking, no abandonment of the self.

The Gospel says eternal life is 'to know you, the only true God, and Jesus Christ whom you have sent' (John 17:3). This is the only revolution that can work, because it begins by challenging that persistent 'I' and all its plans for itself. 'When you were young,' said Jesus to Peter, 'you put on your own belt and walked where you liked; but when you grow old you will stretch out your hands, and somebody else will put a belt around you and take you where you would rather not go' (John 21:18).

Transformation

'It is only in romantic novels that people undergo a sudden change,' wrote Isadora Duncan. 'In real life, even after the most terrible experiences, the main character remains exactly the same.' I have met people I went to school with forty years ago and found that some of them had changed hardly at all, not even in appearance; they were the same as before, only older, and sometimes the effect was comical: they looked like wizened schoolboys. (And they, no doubt, had the same thought about me.) Why, despite all the change around us, do we change so little?

I will say it straight away: I believe we change little because we let go of so little. We are made constantly new by what we let go of, and we are kept the same by what we hold onto. Those wizened schoolboys had taken few risks in their lives, I think; their faces said calculation, calculation of profit; in other words, change only by accumulation. But change by accumulation is not really change, it is just more of the same. A real change involves letting go of a whole structure; it only happens when you truly risk yourself; it is a transformation.

We will all be utterly transformed in the end.... In death we will lose everything we have, we will even lose our very bodies, and much more. And we will not be able to sue anyone for the loss! It seems so unjust! We will be transformed. But how will we let go of everything if we can't even let go of 50p now without knowing that we got full value for it? It would be useful to practise letting go of things, to get in some practice shots before the end. Why not go a little crazy for Christ's sake (like St Paul)? Give things away. No cast-offs, thank you! – that's not giving, that's dumping! I know a woman who cannot even dump her rubbish; she thinks she should be able to sell it. A little thought on her last end would help so much: in the end we will all be unsaleable rubbish. I read that the value of the minerals in a dead body is about 50p, but it would not be economical to extract them. So, our final 50p-worth, at any rate, will go for nothing.

Possession is full of contradictions: what you own owns you, unless you own it as though you did not own it. We know this. Many a man spends a lifetime gathering wealth in order to be happy and secure, only to realise that the tables were turned years ago, inch by inch, and his wealth now owns him: he worries about it, he suspects everyone of wanting to steal it or trick him out of it, and he avoids (and eventually loses) friends who might want to beg it or borrow it; he is its slave and it leaves him no peace. Strangely, it is only when you can give something away that you really own it: till that moment it owns you; you are possessed by your possessions.

All this is clear, perhaps boringly clear; but if it is true of possessions, it is still more true of oneself: I possess myself only when I can give myself away, 'the one who loses his life saves it.' This is quoted with great frequency; what does it mean in practice? What does it mean to give oneself away? For a start, I think, it means to give one's time. (What is time? It is yourself. What do you give when you give someone an hour of your time? You give an hour of yourself.) Then there is the question of quality: you would not want to dump your rubbish on someone else, giving away only the hours that you find useless and unbearable. You want to give people the best hours you have; you give the best of yourself away. Then like water that flows, your being will always be fresh. You will never become stagnant, you will not become a wizened schoolboy, you will be constantly transformed.

'My dear, we live in an age of transition,' said Adam to Eve as they departed from Eden. They left everything behind, and it is still held against them. Yet the Easter Liturgy calls their downfall 'a happy fault,' *felix culpa*. It is called happy because the redemption, the remedy, was better than the original condition. Now if the original great loss can be so called, why not every subsequent loss too? What an antiphon for one's whole life: *Felix culpa!*

How do we change?

> To come to the possession that you have not
> you must go by the way in which you possess not.
> To come to be what you are not,
> you must go by a way in which you are not.
>
> (St John of the Cross)

To put it at its lowest, if you want to move from one armchair to another you will have to deprive yourself of the comfort of all armchairs while you walk across the room. If you cannot endure that privation you will never move from the first armchair, even if the springs are broken and it smells of cat. All change, even change for the better, is renunciation; and if you are afraid of renunciation you will never change.

Or you may be a restless person. Unlike the other who never wants to change, you cannot stop changing; you find your rest only in movement. This too is fuelled by fear, no less than the first. Here too the price of freedom is renunciation: renounce the impulse to move, and be still.

If we ever thought that conservatives were people who wanted to change nothing, while progressives wanted to change everything, we know now that it is not so simple. Personal conversion is a challenge to everyone. You may call yourself a conservative and yet want to change everything to fit in with your own immobility (I have seen many such people). Or you may call yourself progressive and yet be unwilling to change anything in your own outlook or your way of life. The one attitude may be as wilful as the other, and nobody has a corner on enlightenment. There is no good class of people and no bad class; the Gospel makes an urgent call to conversion, addressed to our personal inertia. If you remember your school physics: inertia is the quality of remaining a) in a state of rest, or b) in a state of continuous motion in a straight line. Whatever state a body happens to be in, rest or motion, it remains in that state until knocked out of it by another body. In that sense, all bodies are 'lazy', even the ones that are moving.

All human beings, you could say, are conservative, even the progressive ones. It is 'normal' to be resistant to personal change at a deep level. But the Gospel call to 'Repent and believe the good news' is addressed precisely to that deep-lying resistance in each person, and not to some group or class of people whom we can comfortably call 'those others'. It is normal to assume, when we read the parables of the New Testament, that we are the good group and those others are the bad.

This cocksureness is the proof that we have not heard properly. We assume that the father of the Prodigal Son is running down the road towards us, but in the story he is running to embrace someone else! – the outsider, the waster, the non-serious person who is not 'one of us.' There is rejoicing in heaven over the lost sheep that has been found, but it may not be about me. Or taking myself to be one of the wise virgins I may well be surprised to find the door shut in my face. It is easier than I think to be on the wrong side.

St John of the Cross teaches that I must 'leave myself in everything.' This means: leave behind the self-centred world of the ego, leave behind the urge to promote myself, leave behind every 'gaining' idea I have. Lose interest in myself in the right way. Only then am I truly a free man or woman.

In this nakedness, your spirit
finds its rest; for when it
covets nothing, nothing
raises it up, and nothing
weighs it down, because it stands
in the centre of its humility.

The wisdom of the world tells me that I will be free only if I can build up capital, have connections with influential people and become somehow untouchable, invulnerable. But this other wisdom speaks to me of humility, renunciation, repentance. It tells me I will never be free till I am free of myself, nor will I know how to change anything in myself or be changed; tragedies, joys, big and small events will all leave me untouched. And I will have a deeply ingrained habit of always defending myself and my larger ego: my group, my country, my religion. My God!

Going to the end

There are expressions in ordinary language that convey a sense (perhaps more than a hope) that changes in our lives are not simply random. 'My luck will turn,' we say, even though there is no reason why it should, nor could we even suggest one if we were asked. 'Things have to get worse before they get better,' we say; but why should they not just continue to get worse? Either we sense something hardly perceptible, or we are incurable optimists. Is it nothing more than optimism?

I once gave lumps of clay to a group of people and asked them to make shapes that represented their severest suffering. One young woman made a man's head, with a large mouth. As she worked on it, the mouth got bigger and bigger till the head began to look like that painting called 'The Scream' by Munch. Unlike the painting, however, this was not a nervous scream but a domineering yell. The mouth continued to get absurdly bigger till it dominated the whole head ... bigger and bigger until, to her own amazement (and to mine, as I happened to be looking), everything came out through the mouth, and the whole piece turned itself right inside out! Later in the evening she told me that she had come to some kind of peace in regard to her father. I asked her if this was connected with what we had seen happen to her lump of clay. She said yes, but could not say how. Nor did she need to be able to explain it; what mattered was that a change for the better had taken place in her. It seemed so very like those hunches embedded in ordinary language....

What sense can we make of this? Let us try and explore it. We spend most of our time, I think, like nervous drivers, pulling back from events we fear may challenge or hurt us. But when we see the worst we know that there is nothing worse beyond it; then there is a strange kind of peace: 'you can't fall off the floor.' When something goes to the end, it cannot get worse; it can only get better. Then our mind begins to think of the return journey, the healing. Have you noticed what new life people have when they start putting their lives together again after a tragedy? Could it be that one of the reasons why we feel so little new life in us – one of the reasons we change so little – is that we seldom go to the end of anything? We seldom allow ourselves even to think about the end of anything. Yet all around us in nature we see how change happens: day and night change into each other by going to the end of themselves. Likewise the seasons: they do not hold back and try and stay in the middle, they go to the very end. But we are afraid, usually, to come to the end of anything: a job, a stage of one's life, a relationship, a habit.... We are afraid that we might cease to exist if we changed in any way.

We celebrate the birth of Christ in the very depth of winter, and this is deliberately symbolic, because no one knows what time of year he was born. The Christian feast grafted itself onto the pagan celebration of the Unconquered Sun. At the winter solstice, December the 22nd, when the sun seems ready to vanish completely from the skies, we begin to see the rising of the new Sun, Christ, the Light of the World.

THREE

Fear of Time and Death

Fear and Patsy Fagan

I grew up with a cat named Patsy Fagan, usually just called Fagan. Being known by his surname gave him a certain weight, in my eyes; it put him in the company of the very few in the village who had that distinction. He was weighty enough as it was; I could barely lift him (we were more or less the same size, in my earliest memory). He was also the laziest cat around, never having been known in adult life to do anything quick or energetic, so he consented readily to being carried places. Once, on a hike across the garden, I wanted to let him see his face in a tub of water (he was not only big, but handsome). As I held him over it, suddenly he exploded into life: every ounce of his body turned to pure energy as he leaped away from me, scratching me badly as he did so. I remember the shock of surprise (for he was not only big and handsome but always civil, up to that point.)

Where did all that uncharacteristic energy come from? It came, of course, from fear. If I had been thinking that fear was a property of mice rather than cats, I had to change my opinion there and then. Mice are small and timid-looking and always running away, and they look as if they would prefer to be even smaller; so they have become a symbol of fear. But Fagan proved to me that big, handsome, reposeful people are not exempt from it either. And not only that: fear can give people more energy than they ever had in their lives.

All fear, some wise man said, is fear of death. This is a typical human exaggeration. It is true that whether we have nine lives or only one, we want to protect the precious gift with everything we have. The trouble is we tend to protect it so well that we hardly allow ourselves to live it. And so, fear, which was meant to be our friend, protecting us from harm, becomes instead an enemy, preventing us from doing anything, good or bad. That immense energy that fear generates is turned against oneself, and the effect can be like the immobility of death itself. It must be this that gave that wise man his idea.

Fagan could have put him right. Animals are far more rational in their instincts than we are, by and large. Fagan experienced fear only when there was present danger – exactly according to the teaching of St Thomas Aquinas – otherwise he never wasted a thought on it. Dogs are easily corrupted, they take on our neuroses; but cats are incorruptible, they have much to teach us, and I have always been grateful that my first teacher was Patsy Fagan. He was very sound on most things, sounder than some of the teachers I had later on, and almost as sound as Toby. I will never forget his lesson on fear: he was not ashamed to be afraid when there was present danger, but about absent dangers he couldn't care less.

Generalised fear leads to uncertainty about who you are: you are forever pulling back, not daring, escaping rather. All this is backwardness, in a literal sense. Time goes forward, so if you are always pulling back does it surprise you that you don't know who you are? Make it a rule always to go forward (except when there is present danger), and you will know who you are. Soon, you may even be able to go forward into the teeth of present danger. There have been great Christians who could do that. But begin by going forward into the teeth of absent dangers! There was a man who said on his deathbed, 'I had a lot of trouble in my life ... oh, such a lot; but most of it never happened.'

I once heard it said that God made cats so that we could have the pleasure of stroking the tiger. Inside every cat, even the likes of the languid Fagan, there is an incorruptible wild beast, friend of solitude and of the night, of a purity of instinct that we have lost forever. They show us in a poor light, and many people secretly resent them for this. Instead why not give admiration where it is due? Stroke the cat and be in awe of the tiger: the sleek movement, the perfection, the speed. (Fagan would have moved fast more than once if there had been sufficient reason.) Learn about fear and the handling of fear: how not to turn your own energy against yourself, how to live forwards instead of backwards, how to ignore absent dangers, how to learn who you are ... and how not to be resentful when one of God's uncorrupted creatures teaches you these lessons. You wanted a professor, did you, to teach you these things? Well, Fagan or any of his kind can be your professor.

Fear and faith

The hall of your house is so nice and proper; and the front room is kept so well. All the right pictures are hanging there, the carpets are clean, the furniture nicely arranged. This is the route for visitors who are not really part of your life. But your friends come in the back door, directly into the kitchen. That is the place where everything happens: not only the cooking, but all the talking and laughing and the arguments; it is the place where the family really lives. It is often a bit of a mess, but when you are there you know you are home. Still, front and back are parts of the same house; the front door and the back door are two valid approaches to the one family home.

It is so with many things in our faith: you can approach from the front or from the back. What I want to say now is that the front door and hall of your house are like the Creed we recite at Mass (everything is correct, nothing is missing); but if you want to know what is really happening in your house of faith, approach by the back door: look at your fears. In the New Testament, the opposite of faith is a certain kind of fear: not the natural instinct of fear, and not the fear that is a gift of the Holy Spirit, but a kind of neurotic fear that immobilises you, that wants nothing to happen, good or bad.

Hundreds of times I have asked groups of people, young and old, to write down their fears. It is a useful thing to do, for while you are writing down your fears you are looking at them, and that is always the first step towards living wisely with them. I always asked people not to sign their names, and I always asked their permission to read those pieces of paper to the whole group afterwards. I found over the years that the three greatest fears were death, loneliness and the unknown. But two of these were double: death was sometimes one's own death and sometimes the death of someone near; and the unknown was sometimes the 'spooky' unknown and sometimes simply the future. That makes a list of five: one's own death, the death of someone close, loneliness, the future and the spooky side of life. I always got this list, not from every person without fail (human beings are not predictable even in this) but with remarkable regularity. Of course, even when such lists are almost identical, the human experience always has a salty individual taste.

Beyond these common five fears there are many others, of course. There are purely individual fears occasioned by some event in a person's life, but there are other common ones, I found: some that are distinctive of men and boys, and others of women and girls. Again, not with full regularity nor to the exclusion of the other group, I found that men and boys very frequently have a great fear of making a wrong decision; while women and girls very frequently have a fear of the four elements – fire, air, earth and water: fear of being trapped in a burning building, for example, or of being suffocated, or buried alive or drowned. No doubt, if you asked a man whether he would experience fear in a burning building, he would say yes, but the point is that he seldom thinks of it when you do not ask. I have often asked myself what this difference means. I do not know the answer; perhaps it has something to do with male wilfulness and women's more thorough incarnation.

I recommend this exercise: in a quiet moment, find a piece of paper and a pencil and write down at random (without thinking too much about it, in case you rationalise it) a full list of all your fears, no matter how particular. It has the following benefits. While you are doing that you are looking at them, and as I said earlier, that is the first step in making peace with them. Fears usually take hold of you by the back, when you are running away from them. But when you face them, they diminish; they are like cowardly dogs. It will also help you to see where your faith is, at the moment. Fear and faith are opposites, so when you locate your fear you have also located the spot where faith has work to do.

We recite the Creed every week; it would be useful to recite occasionally the list of our fears, to see what's cooking in the kitchen.

Anxiety

The word 'anxiety' comes from the Latin *angere*, which means 'to choke'. This expresses exactly the self-defeating nature of anxiety: just at the moment of stress when you would need to breathe fully and freely, you feel choked. It is like having a drowning man's grip on your own throat. What is the difference between anxiety and fear? It is a matter of particular usage; people tend to use the word 'anxiety' in preference to 'fear' when it is a question of unlocated fear – a vague disquiet that goes looking for a reason to be fearful when there is none to hand. Or it is used to refer to impotent fear: when there is nothing you can do, when even running away is useless – because everything is out of your hands. If anxiety stays with you habitually it becomes part of you; it gets to be like a second skin, coming between you and everything.

There are degrees of anxiety, from slight nervousness to complete paralysis. It is not always a bad thing to be a little nervous: it sharpens you up, it makes you alert and attentive. But it becomes a problem when it makes you so conscious of danger that you are aware of nothing else. Then you cannot move, you lose your rational power, you are like a dazzled rabbit. 'The Age of Anxiety' our age has been called. If our faith has something to say to this age, then it must have something to say to us about anxiety.

Our faith is a way of salvation, that is, literally, a way of being saved. Does this mean that it encourages us to play safe in every

situation? Hardly. Jesus never played safe in his life. And listen
for a while, if it is not too much, to St Paul's account of his own
life: 'I have been sent to prison ... and whipped so many times,
often almost to death. Five times I had the thirty-nine lashes
from the Jews; three times I have been beaten with sticks; once
I was pelted with stones; three times I have been shipwrecked
and I was once adrift on the open sea for a night and a day.
Constantly travelling, I have been in danger from rivers and in
danger from brigands, in danger from my own people and in
danger from pagans; in danger in the towns, in danger in the
open country, danger at sea and danger from so-called brothers.
I have worked and laboured, often without sleep; I have been
hungry and thirsty and often starving; I have been in the cold
without clothes. And, to leave out much more, there is my daily
preoccupation: my anxiety for all the churches' (2 Corinthians
11:23-28). Clearly, for Paul faith does not mean playing safe. It is
not a means of avoiding problems and suffering but rather a way
of going through them.

If you try to avoid fear by avoiding problems, you will still be
left with your fear: you will live in fear that the problems will
catch up with you when you least expect it. In this way, ordinary
fear will turn into anxiety, a generalised fear that will never leave
you alone. It is better to face the music once and be done with
it. We will never have a problem-free existence, and if we had,
it would not be good for us. What we need is a way of facing
problems that does not turn our natural fear into anxiety. Why
not learn from an expert, the man who gave us that litany of
hardships that I quoted? He gives us this surprising key: 'I shall
be very happy to make my weaknesses my special boast so that
the power of Christ may stay over me, and that is why I am quite
content with my weaknesses, and with insults, hardships,
persecutions, and the agonies I go through for Christ's sake. For
it is when I am weak that I am strong' (2 Corinthians 12:10).

Our greatest difficulty in facing problems is that we think we
have to be tough. But if you were tough you would be more likely
to create further problems, not only for others but for yourself!

There is no one so breakable as the man who thinks he is tough.
Just look around. It is a wrong formula. Go in, instead, with an
open vulnerable heart. You may come out limping, like Jacob
who wrestled with the angel. But like him you will have received
a blessing (Genesis 32:25-29).

Redeeming the time

If you are walking down the street (said the elderly gentleman to
me) and you stop just anywhere, you can say that the street is
divided into two parts: the part you have travelled and the part
you have yet to travel. But it makes no difference to the street;
the street is the same before you and behind. Likewise with time,
he said: the past and the future are all the one, and we make too
much of the difference between them. If something is true, it is
true in the past and future equally. Time is not important, it is
superficial; it is the eternal that counts. You are relatively young,
he said; when you are my age you will understand.

   On the surface this sounded very religious, but one should
always be suspicious of 'timeless' religion. I was slow to disagree
with such a venerable old man; but when he told me he had been
reading Bertrand Russell's *Mysticism and Logic*, I took courage;
it was not like disputing his own thoughts.

   'Time is an unimportant and superficial characteristic of
reality,' Russell had written (and he experienced a lot of time:
ninety-seven years of it). 'To realise the unimportance of time is
the gate of wisdom.... ' When Russell used the words 'contemplation' and 'the eternal world' (as he did repeatedly in that
book) we may be tempted to see this as a religious affirmation,
but it was no such thing; Russell did not believe in the existence
of any God: in fact he gave atheism an extra sharp cutting edge.
Many 'timeless' approaches to reality look religious, when in fact
they are quite the opposite; it is certainly hard to see how a
rejection of time could be Christian. The Word of God became
flesh, according to our religion, entering the world of time and
embracing it to the very end, to death and beyond. How could

we reject time when Christ was born in time, lived and died in time? To try to have a 'timeless' religion is to cut off Christ; his incarnation tells us to look to the world of time and not to try and short-circuit ourselves into eternity.

The gentleman overruled this objection. Time scatters everything, he said; it is like the wind; we are constantly being borne away from the past, from friends ... and even from ourselves, for it is time that bears us to the grave. To live in this world is to lose more and more until eventually we have lost everything. Time and death are one; every moment that passes is a kind of death, it will never return and live again; we die a little every day. 'How could our religion be about time?' he exclaimed. Surely it is about getting above time. Long ago his grandmother used to recite: 'This world is but a passing show, / Deceitful joy, deceitful woe; / There's nothing true but heaven.' It is no less true now than then, he said, for time has nothing to do with it.

It is no wonder, I said (with respect), that with that attitude to time you have to look for something else. If time makes no difference to truth, then your old age gives you no advantage, so I make bold to disagree. (Dignity rubs off on you, doesn't it? You could never say 'Rubbish!' to such a man.) How painful to say our life is a progressive loss! But true! he interjected. True and false, said I. You will have to make a choice between these two, I'm afraid, he said. It is true, said I, that we lose more and more, and we will eventually be 'sans teeth, sans eyes, sans taste, sans everything.' But to speak of losing what we have is surely negative and defeatist. Instead, we should speak of giving everything away. In John's Gospel, when Jesus said on the cross, 'It is finished!' this did not mean, 'I have been defeated!' It meant just the opposite: 'I have achieved it!' 'He yielded up his spirit,' the Gospel says; it was not torn from him. Likewise death does not defeat us, it is something we achieve ... ! Perhaps?

When I stopped he said, 'Proceed!' (Oh for old manners!) Strange that someone who had grown old so beautifully should have such negative things to say about the experience of time and ageing. I hope it was only a passing indisposition caused by reading *Mysticism and Logic*. But I proceeded. Business people say time is money, but we know that time is priceless: it cannot be bought for love nor money. It has been redeemed by Christ from meaninglessness. We say 'redeemed', which means 'bought back': a business term, yes, but this only reflects our preoccupation with business; we are like the man whose only question about everything is, 'How much?' The reality itself – what the incarnation has done to time – is mysterious and beyond all business. Time is priceless; each moment is a unique and priceless gem. This makes it a perfect gift; it also makes it a perfect object of greed. These are the two attitudes that people have to gems. We can give our time away like someone conferring gems on a beautiful woman, or we can rush down the street, shouting, 'I've been robbed!'

He made some response that was so well-bred, so perfectly neutral, that I retained no memory of it. Then he took out a smooth gold watch from his waistcoat pocket, looked at its face and said, 'Bertrand Russell,' as if reading the name there. He tapered off the conversation, excused himself politely and departed. I never found out what he meant by Bertrand Russell.

Midlife

> As for man, his days are like grass;
> he flowers like the flower of the field;
> the wind blows and he is gone
> and his place never sees him again. (Psalm 102)

Few young people can really know what these lines are about: you have to know the bitter-sweet taste of limited time, that knowledge approaching mathematical certainty that you have already lived more than half your life. That bitter-sweet taste gives you a depth, or a capacity for depth, that nothing else could give. Dante's *Divina Commedia* begins, 'In the middle of life's journey....'

It is no second-hand knowledge, this knowledge of mortality;

you have to live fifty years to attain it, and when you do, it is not abstract knowledge but an inseparable part of your being. You are not like the person who knows 'the price of everything and the value of nothing.' For the first time in your life, it seems, you know what is valuable and what is valueless. For the first time you see the shape of your life: there is enough of it in place to let you guess the probable shape of the whole (with due allowance for surprises). When you were young you felt as if your life would never end: everything you did and thought had unlimited horizons. In midlife the horizon has come near; in certain moments you feel you could reach out and touch it. The young live a kind of eternity, but you are learning about time.

It is remarkable how many time-machines there are in science-fiction. H.G. Wells invented the prototype, and there have been many imitations. Time-travel is an abiding fascination. Dr Who and the likes of him could travel to any century in the past or future. It is a dream of simultaneity, a wish that we could have it all together: past, present and future. It is an attempt to fashion a spurious eternity out of time. How hard it is at any time, but especially when we are young, to be certain that our days are like grass.

Not only science fiction.... Even our involvement with photography can be seen as a kind of search for eternity. 'The need to bring things spatially and humanly "nearer" is almost an obsession today,' wrote Walter Benjamin. The most distant parts of the world, and also the past, can be 'captured' on film and so made present here and now. Mediaeval philosophers, following Boethius, described eternity as 'the perfect possession, without duration, of endless life.' Without duration: they used the words *tota simul*, which mean 'all at once' or 'all together'. All together: like photography. Photography: an aspect of our search for *tota simul*, for eternity.

Yet time passes, never to return, and so do we. We can deny our age, but no denial will stem the tide. See the long hairs combed from far and wide to shroud the pitiful bald patch: how the man must live in dread of sudden gusts! See the mini-skirted lady with tumbling blonde hair, and see all the more clearly the evidence of years that no art can hide. Why engage in a battle that cannot be won, in which you are driven back inch by inch? Why define your life as a continual defeat? Why not say: I will not consider that I am being pushed out of my life; I will choose instead to walk into it, moment by moment. Time cannot be stopped, cannot be captured and held. It comprehends us, in the strict sense of the word: it encloses us and extends beyond us; we do not comprehend it. We have to let go of that spurious eternity (it is the struggle of midlife) in order to know our immersion in time – to know the very taste of it. It may well be the most difficult journey of our life.

> In the middle of life's journey
> I found myself in a dark wood
> Where the right road was lost.

La diritta via: the right road, the direct route, the straight path. Youth is the time for straight solutions; in midlife begins the complexity: time itself. In Jesus, our God leaped into human time (all of it, including death) so that we would learn not to despise it, or feel trapped in it, or try to flee from it into imagined eternities of our own, false eternities that are no more than a denial of time – in other words, no more than a fear of death. Our faith tells us to love the gift of time that God gives us: to love every part of it, youth, middle age, old age; to love the ripening, the mellowing and the deepening that come with the passing years....

We think that loving something means capturing it and killing it. 'What a beautiful flower, let me pluck it!' – in other words, cut its head off, kill it. 'What a beautiful sight, let me take a photo of it!'

How are we to love time? By not trying to stop it, but by letting it pass. With a glad heart let it pass. Then death will not come as an enemy.

What might have been

What I could have become but did not: that is the insolvency, the embarrassing shortfall that I can never now make up. (When I say 'I', I mean you too!) If I regret many things I did in the past, I have far greater reason to regret all the things I left undone. In fantasy I could have become a famous surgeon, a still more famous athlete, a household name to millions; but I can leave that alone because I know it is just fantasy. What I cannot so easily leave alone is the thought that I could have achieved many things that fell (or would have fallen, with effort) within my reach, but I simply did not. This is one of the painful thoughts that beset men and women in their middle years. In earlier life we could still say that we were only postponing, that we would get around to all those things later on. And in old age we will have come to terms, we hope, with the past and learned to live with our regrets. But the first painful onset, the knowledge of limitation, is in midlife.

Let me draw out the pain of it a little more (this hurts me more than it hurts you!) I know I am limited; I was born in a particular time and place, I had particular parents and upbringing and schooling, I was not exposed to everything. I can accept that. Even Jesus, the Word made flesh, was limited in that way; he was known as Jesus of Nazareth. For example, he had a country accent: the city people who stood watching as he died thought he was saying 'Eli' when he said 'Eloi'. So I can't complain about the given limitations of my life; over these I had no control. What is harder is to know that I added spectacularly to them. Will it be true of me too that I was 'born a man and died a shopkeeper?' I hung back from opportunities and challenges, I preferred beaten tracks though I had the power to open up new ones, I was lazy and unimaginative; and now I am the net result of all that. I am like a gambler whose luck has run out and who can no longer honour his debts.

Have we had enough? There's more! There is not only the thought of what I could have become and did not; there is also the thought of what I once was, but am now no longer. The memory is no longer sharp, several interests have died, the cutting edge of one's life is blunted.

We might as well plunge to the bottom now! There is not only the thought of what I can no longer do; there is the more grievous thought that everything I ever did was meaningless. Yes, this is on the menu too! What can I do with it? For a start I can take comfort in the thought that I am not alone in this. Meet Qoheleth. He will keep us company in our present mood. 'I did great things (he said): I built houses and planted vineyards. I made gardens and fields and planted all kinds of fruit trees. I constructed reservoirs to irrigate the orchards.... I acquired silver and gold. I enjoyed all that I undertook, and that was my reward for my work.... Then I considered all I had achieved by my work and all the labour it had entailed, and I found that it was all meaningless and chasing the wind' (Qoheleth 2:4-11).

What redemption is there for this havoc that time wreaks on us all? There is hope, we know, for all truthful experiences; it is only lies that lead nowhere.

> Through all the lying days of my youth
> I swayed my leaves and flowers in the sun;
> Now I may wither into the truth. (W.B. Yeats)

There is hope, is there not, in the fact that these experiences find expression in great literature and in the Scriptures? They are not just a modern neurosis, then. They are a constant in human experience, they have to do with the truth of our life, and they open us to the God of truth.

Promise

His was a stark view. 'Watch people passing in the city,' he said. 'All are in hot pursuit of one thing or another. Look at them, most of them are running. Use your imagination to fill in what is invisible. Imagine that you can see the things they are pursuing. What would you see? Bags of groceries, buses, appointments.... That list of things is their future. There! – that is the reason they think it worth while to endure the present.'

But the only future you see on the street, I objected, is the immediate future; everything on the street is a sweaty *now*. People have longer futures that they give themselves to when they cross their own thresholds and put down their parcels.

'Do they?' he shot in. 'Do they? I'll tell you what most of them do: they switch on the television in order to be mentally back on the street. The street has invaded the home now, to the point that home exists no more; everything is a vast street, and the only future that most people think about is the immediate future. The world is now exactly inside out: stories that belong in the kitchen and bedroom are scattered all over the city by the media, while the home itself has become a street! The house has emptied itself into the street, and the street into the house.'

It was a relief to escape from his intensity. I watched him board his bus along with all the other creatures of the immediate future, and he looked no different from them; he was another passenger fumbling for his ticket. He looked frail, intense and distracted. For all his generalities he looked particular – just as particular as the rest. It is not possible really to step outside humanity and judge it. We are inside, not outside. He said the world was turning inside out, but he is involved in the same thing himself: he is inside but he is pretending to be outside – and he is judging us, moralising over us.

In Hebrew the verb tenses are not as in English. We take the arrangement of past, present and future tenses in English for granted, but there are people who arrange things differently. God said to Moses, 'I am who I am,' but I have seen this translated as 'I will be who I will be.' Perhaps our modern languages give us too much clarity in some ways, a false clarity. Are the past and future so cleanly shaven from the present that a second ago – or a millisecond – is simply the past and a second from now the future? Surely this is about the infinite divisibility of numbers, and not about our experience of living our lives. In living experience I am not just my present instant; I am also my past and my future. (I know the danger of making alibis of the past and future, but this need not panic me into a microscopic 'now'.) In our own way we too can say, 'I am who I am,' and it also means 'I will be who I will be.' I am my hopes and promises. To live in the face of them is not to escape into the future; it is to face what I am. An ultimate future faces every person. By this I mean that the question, What do I ultimately hope for from this life? is an inescapable question now. ('Ultimate' does not mean last of all; in this context it means first or fundamental.) I also mean that the question, What do I ultimately promise? is likewise inescapable.

Especially when we are young we don't like to make long promises, yet we want life to promise us everything. Long-term promises like marriage or religious profession are seen as reckless. The media have given everything an air of absolute urgency; everything is a nearly microscopic now; there is no time for a real future in which to hope and promise. We are becoming less capable of the most noble thing we can say to one another and to God: I promise. The Genesis verse did not mean 'I will be' in the abstract; it meant 'I will be for you.' For you I will be who I will be.

I need to give myself profoundly to the future; that is part of what it is to love time, to love life itself. Love casts out fear. If I can be courageous in the face of the future, then when my future comes it will be mine. And only when it is mine can I give it away. To God and to others. For you I will be who I will be.

Madonna of Durres

I worked for a short time in Albania with Mother Teresa's Sisters. The shock of seeing a devastated country is still vivid. In Albanian the country is called *Shqiperi* (pronounced 'shippery'), which means Land of the Eagle. But fifty years of Enver Hoxha's Stalinist regime shot that eagle well and truly out of the sky. A beautiful country was reduced to a bunker – or rather seven hundred thousand bunkers; they dot the countryside like mushrooms. The cost of building them was the gross national product for twenty-five years, yet they served no purpose whatever. The master-bunker must have been the mind of the dictator himself. The repression was total: I met a young man who served a prison sentence for humming an Italian tune. There were heavy prison sentences for owning an extra animal.... Towards the end, people were starving. Once the regime fell, international aid began to pour in. A woman told me that she saw a relief truck being hijacked by a crowd of men: they forced it to stop, then having wrenched the doors open they stood around eating the bread that it was carrying!

If Albania seems very far away, this is only because it was a closed country for so long: nothing could get in or out. But in fact it is only one hour's flight from Rome. It was the ancient Illyricum, a division of the Roman Empire. I stayed in the port city of Durres, where most of the classical remains were bulldozed to make way for the works of a dictator's ego. A few things remain, however: one is an amphitheatre – a Colosseum equal in size to the one in Rome. The difference is that it lies half buried and neglected. Over the parts that are not excavated there are tangles of houses from various centuries; but where some excavation has been roughly done, you can walk through the arches of the amphitheatre at the original ground level and imagine that you were walking in Illyricum.

Two of those deep arches were used as small Christian churches in Byzantine times. They are in ruins, of course, because the regime tolerated no religion; and now that the regime has fallen, the dominant religion, as before, is Islam. As I leaped over puddles of water (the country was still being scourged when I was there, but only with terrible weather) I saw fragments of painting, frescoes, on the saturated walls. As I looked carefully and my eyes became accustomed to the dark I saw a wide-open eye looking straight at me. It was a startling moment of recognition, like meeting your mother or your sister unexpectedly a thousand miles from home. If anything ever moved me deeply it was that partial face with its large eye,

looking across a thousand years at us and our devastated world.
It was the face of a tenth century fresco of Mary. For me it had
to be a Madonna of Compassion (everyone's mother, I suppose,
is a madonna of compassion, and we don't know how to describe
her objectively). The Madonna came to birth there 'in midst of
other woe than ours,' but she embraces with compassion all the
yearning and sighing generations. Nor is hers an easy compassion from a safe place: she is the *Mater dolorosa*, the mother of
sorrows, and here on this damp wall her image is wasting; one
day its last fragments will fall away, and few will notice or care.
The ruined chapel is not protected in any way: there is no gate,
no caretaker, no guide; it is totally vulnerable to vandalism,
neglect and dampness. It is a spark of light that may be
extinguished at any moment.

In a small cluttered room where someone had put piles of
antiques found lying around (My God! Ancient Illyricum
reduced to this!) a woman showed me glass funerary urns from
the first and second centuries. Inside them were tiny glass phials,
for holding the tears of the bereaved wife or mother. Then she
showed me earthenware urns, for the ashes of the poor. Inside
these were earthenware phials, much larger than the glass ones.
'The poor have more tears, you see,' she said.

Compassion is not from a safe place; it does not protect itself
behind steel bars and glass. 'Thou silent form,' said Keats of the
Grecian urn, 'dost tease us out of thought / as doth eternity.' But
those tears shed long ago, and the silent Madonna, tease us
instead into thought and into time, into the particular, because
they are mother images. We need to know more of God's
motherhood: otherwise we will find that we have put ourselves
and our faith behind steel bars and glass ... and bunkers.

Fear of the end

I asked a group of people to give shape to their fears – in clay.
Children do this, without any instruction. There is some
wisdom in looking straight at the things that terrify us. Within

half an hour the table was covered with 'shapes': that is the only word that could include them all. There were many indecipherable shapes that could mean nothing except to their makers. There were many shapes of the expected kind: horrible beasts, skulls, coffins, dragons.... What surprised me was the great number of snakes. But when you reflect on it, it is quite a traditional theme.

The snake is an important figure in the symbolism of many religions, including that of the Old and New Testaments. It has different meanings, one being 'enemy of God':

> The Lord will punish with the sword …
> Leviathan the gliding serpent,
> Leviathan the coiling serpent (Isaiah 27:1).

When the Chosen People began to complain on their long journey out of Egypt, ('the house of slavery'), when they began to wish they had not been persuaded to embark on that long trek through the desert to the Promised Land, God let the ancient enemy have a go at them, to teach them a lesson. 'The Lord sent venomous snakes among them; they bit the people and many Israelites died.' This stopped them complaining about the food. 'There is no bread!' they had been saying, 'there is no water! and we detest this miserable food!' They liked the snakes even less, so they asked Moses to intercede for them. The Lord said to Moses, 'Make a snake and put it up on a pole; anyone who is bitten can look at it and live' (Numbers 21:8).

This is very strange, and no doubt it reflects the variety of meanings that snakes had in ancient mythology. One of those meanings was 'fertility', which suggests vigorous health, and therefore 'healer'. (To this day the snake is the symbol of the medical profession.) But etymology doesn't explain anything, and it often needs to be explained itself. Why should looking at a snake be a cure for snake-bite? Who knows what deep intuitions made this connection?

Move on many centuries and you find the writer of the fourth Gospel looking back at that event in the desert and seeing a profound meaning in it. 'Just as Moses lifted up the snake in the desert, so the Son of Man must be lifted up, that everyone who believes in him may have eternal life' (John 3:14).

Look at the very things, we are being told, that terrify you. It is important, above all else, to look at death, 'the prince of terrors.'

It is not as if salvation were being reduced to a psychological trick. Far from it. But the human reality of fear is always with us; we have to live with it, knowing that it can cripple us if we do not learn how to regard it wisely. We can be grateful for that first insight: look at the things that cause you fear. We have an instinct to look away, but fear attacks us even more effectively when we do that.

Still, the Scriptures are more than psychology; they are a word of life. Jesus said, 'I came that you may have life,' not 'that you may learn to cope.' The last word about fear is not that it is something to cope with, but that it can be a road to life, even eternal life, beyond our imagining. The death of Jesus is the opening out to that life. This changes the scene entirely: death is not a problem but an opening to deeper life. If we insist on using the language of problem and solution, we would have to say here (as always) that the solution should be looked for in the problem; it is not to be found in flight from the problem. Life comes out of death, through death, not despite it or from somewhere else. This is why John can play on the ambiguity of 'lifted up' when he speaks of the death of Jesus: he was lifted up in shame on the Cross, but that was also a lifting up in glory; he was lifted up to die, but that death was the doorway to life.

When we give shape to our fears (in clay, or more usually in words, or in just looking) we are setting out on a path that does not leave us lost in the woods but leads to the very end of the road ... and beyond.

FOUR

Dying to the Ego

What is it?

We should like to know love and freedom and fearlessness in the way you know a tree when you fold your arms around it or climb into its branches. Instead we know them as ideas, or theories, or only words.... But talking and singing about love is not love, thinking about freedom is not freedom, wishing to be fearless is not fearlessness. What is it that robs us of direct knowledge of these and other realities? The ego.

What is the ego? It is an idea. But first of all it is a word. It comes from Latin where it was the ordinary word for 'I'. It has had a long lonely life in modern philosophy and theology, becoming the 'absolute or metaphysical subject' – the world-watcher – but so intellectualised in the end that it was no longer part of the world but only a limit of the world. At a more popular level it has taken on a psychological colouring, referring to one's conscious or self-conscious self. But because this was too close for comfort to the words 'egoistic' and 'egocentric', it now appears simply as 'the self' in the vast literature of self-help, self-actualisation and New Age spirituality. That literature is descended, partly, from the highly individualistic culture of western philosophy and theology, and has the same individualistic slant; it flows in to remedy the deficiencies of modern religion or to fill the vacuum left by its disappearance from many people's lives.

Of course the ego does not exist only in books. Everyone (except mystics) has an ego. What is it? As I said, it is an idea. It is not who you are in reality, but your idea of who you are. This is able to insert itself between you and your reality: a narrow place, but a place where a separation of even a millimetre is disastrous. It is not real itself, but it is able to cause real trouble. It is the very structure of all our problems, and we always have to try and see it with all the clarity we can manage.

First of all, we should not imagine that it is only absent-minded professors who become separated from reality. Can anyone who spends three or four hours every day watching television be in deep contact with reality? Or anyone who lives a life of sexual fantasy, or power fantasy, or violence fantasy? Yes, not only professors: anyone can live in another world!

How do we become separated from our own experience, and so from reality? Consciousness is meant to be consciousness of something else, but we are able to turn it into something for itself, a private kind of entertainment, a way of being mentally occupied without doing anything – without going out of ourselves. For example, when we look at a tree do we see the tree at all? Do we just register the word 'tree', or say something to ourselves about trees in general, or plan something we want to do ('I must cut that down, or lop off that branch'), or quote a few lines from a poem? Very often we do everything except look at it.

It is as if we had a set of cards in our mind and when something out there (a tree) triggers the process we begin to flick through those cards, pausing to glance at one or other of them. All these cards are past experiences; they are memories: of other trees, of old ideas and scraps of language about trees. There is nothing from now, there is nothing new. But while we shuffle those cards we have the feeling that we are in full command of the tree situation. We feel we have accounted for the tree and therefore also for ourselves: we are people who know our way around. But we have not related to the tree at all in fact, we have been playing inside our heads with toys of long ago, we have not gone out of ourselves to the tree, we have continued to be absorbed in the ego, our consciousness has not been of anything real.

In place of trees put people. How terrible to see nothing new in people, to reshuffle a few prejudices in one's mind every time we meet them, to put them in boxes while they are still alive! The ego is related to nothing real, neither things nor people; it is a house of cards.

To see anything or anyone you have to go out of yourself: forget yourself and your house of cards, become a new person every moment. How do you become a new person every moment? By becoming nothing every moment! I know that this sounds peculiar, but wait. If you allowed the ego to plan what kind of new person you were to become moment by moment, you would never be a new person; the ego is always old and second-hand. Instead, go out of yourself so completely, become so fully involved in everything you see and do, that you forget yourself completely; that is what I mean by becoming nothing. When you become nothing moment by moment you become a new person moment by moment.

The ego can pretend to love, can pretend to be free, can pretend to be fearless; but it is just that: a pretence. Only a new person can love, only a new person can be free, only a new person can be fearless moment by moment. The faith we profess assures us that this newness is possible. 'Those who are in Christ are a new creation' (2 Corinthians 5:17).

Who or what am I?

'Why, do you think, is it so hard for us to penetrate to the depths of our souls? The reason is that we are overgrown with so many thick, coarse scales. They are as thick as the skull of an ox, and they have covered up our inner selves so completely that neither God nor we ourselves can get in. There is an impenetrable growth in the way. Some of us have thirty or forty layers of scale there, thick, horny skin like the pelt of a bear.... There are some people so made that whatever one says to them, nothing penetrates.... '

This straight talk was from Johann Tauler in the fourteenth century. If it sounds tough and chunky in English, imagine how it must have sounded in Middle High German! If we always spoke like that, it would be far harder to get above oneself in spirituality. Tauler could teach us to keep our feet on the ground.

Of course, we could have our feet on the literal ground, as every ox does (in fact twice as much as you or I!) and still fail to be in touch with the reality that Tauler is asking us to see. The ego, the false self, comes between. This self is not a solid reality, it is something reflected. From earliest childhood we have seen ourselves reflected in the faces of other people. We have seen that some people like us, some of the time, depending on what we do or say or how we look, or how they happen to feel at the time. At other times they dislike us, for equally arbitrary reasons. We attempt then to form our sense of self-identity out of this mass of contradictory impressions and memories and associations. It is not surprising that we hardly know who we are. But for practical purposes we have to settle it somehow; we have to project a sense of who we are, even when we don't know. So we somehow make a selection of experiences that 'name' us, that tell who we are. That's who I am, we say; that's my personality. It carries a lot of wishful thinking in it, and it is never the whole story; it is the fundamental lie. So, like the fearful person whistling in the dark, or the bully who is really a coward, the ego is a work of fiction. It is very insecure, being a fundamental lie, so we have to defend it, claiming whatever fits in with it and rejecting what does not. In this way it often becomes hard and assertive, 'as thick as the skull of an ox.' The ego is always an unlovely creation, even though it is often designed to be acceptable to others or to impress them. A lie is never beautiful.

Our real identity, our being (Tauler and so many others tell us), is much more difficult to be aware of, because it is cloaked by this other self. Tauler (again like so many others) makes the astonishing statement that our real self is 'a nothingness'. He does not mean it isn't there; he means that to see it is an experience of openness, 'emptiness' in the good sense: not being full of oneself. 'There is a part of the soul,' said Eckhart, 'that is like God, because, like God, it is like nothing.' God is formless and looks therefore like non-being, looks like nothing. It is easy to use words lightly, with little sense of the struggle that there is in all language about God; it is easy also to say light things about our own being, things not based on experience at all. Out of the corner of our eye (or the corner of the mind) we sense that there is a greater depth in us than we know, that our being is somehow a source that does not run dry, and that it is a very pure source if we do not pollute it. It is our being, it comes from God moment by moment. And so, vanity has no part in it, possessiveness has no part in it, it does not have to lie in order to exist, it is from beyond. How strange it is that the deepest and most intimate thing in us should be from beyond. We are mysterious indefinable beings; like God, we are like nothing.

Person, place or thing

Is a person a thing? I don't mean just any old thing; I mean a very special kind of living thing. Or are persons so special that you cannot properly call them things at all? Still, 'You poor thing!' we say to people (and not only children) when we are filled with pity for them. They are not insulted by our choice of words; they are usually consoled. But on the other hand, try *treating* people as things – pushing them around, or ignoring them, or throwing them out – and you get a very different reaction indeed. So, why can't we make up our minds: are we things or are we not?

I'll come back to that. What if we were to think of persons as places? I listened for hours to a person of very strong will who was in constant trouble (with himself as much as with other people) for that very will-power of his. I had the impression of a small ball of steel. From that steel core he had been trying all his life to impose his plans on the world; and when it was not plans it was expectations, which are just as bad. Suddenly I thought to say to him, 'Why not think of yourself as a place, instead of a thing?' He was very surprised: this kind of talk was not according to any plan of his!

I'll come back to him! There are precedents for calling people places. St Paul called us 'temples of the living God' (2 Corinthians

6:16). A temple is a place. In the Litany of Loreto we call Mary
an ark, a house, a vessel, a tower.... All these could be described
as things, of course, but they are just as truly places. Think of
yourself as a place where God is at work, and you will be less
tempted to think that the world's salvation depends on you and
your plans.

The word 'room' (and its German cousin *Raum*) means
'space'. We build a room and then proceed to fill it with clutter,
making it the opposite of a room. But there is a need for empty
space there; if there were no empty space it could no longer be
called a room in a proper sense. It is the same with us: the
essential is to get rid of the clutter in our lives, our hearts, our
minds; the essential is to make room.

The trouble with clutter is that you become so used to it that
you think you cannot do without it. In that sense you become
identified with it. This is even more true of inner clutter than it
is of outer. You become identified with your work, your ideas,
your plans; and if you were ever to be deprived of these, you
would feel that you scarcely existed any more. But of course you
would exist, and you would be more yourself than before. You
would be identified with yourself rather than with your clutter.
You would know the indestructible beauty of emptiness. You
would be a place where God was at work.

Rooms have walls. So have we, walls of some kind: boundaries, limits (and limitations), ways of being private. These walls
are not so stout as the ones of stone or brick; with one word
someone can breach your wall, and with a bit of sustained effort
they can knock it to the ground. This is a disaster if you have
identified yourself with your clutter: it is all exposed to view, it
looks so petty and embarrassing – as household things always do
when a wall is knocked down and they become visible from the
street. But space itself is inviolable. And when all your walls fall
down in death your identity, you believe, will not be dissipated.
In some mysterious way you will be more yourself than ever
before, and there will be no barrier between you and God, nor
between you and others. Then the Spirit will blow where it wills

and you will be rapt up in a mystery beyond imagination. Meditation is when you sit for half an hour or so and live with that detachment from clutter, and you try not to care so much about your walls: you open your mind and heart to God and the world.

In that attitude fear lets go of you, fear that usually makes you feel small and cornered. It unties its traps and releases you into a wider world.... Whenever you want, you can go back to being a thing! Physicists (a race of people, I think, who dislike ambiguity more than most) have to live with ambiguity: they cannot settle the question whether light is particles or waves, so they work with the understanding that it is either, or both. Why should not a Christian (who inherits a profound wisdom about symbolism and language) think, and live, sometimes like a thing and sometimes like a place? Even the steel man has begun to attempt it!

The examined life

'The unexamined life is not liveable for a human being,' wrote Plato twenty five centuries ago. By an unexamined life he meant a life without reflection, without thinking. He forgot to mention that the over-examined life is just as bad. I met a man who was a perfect example of it. He used to hold long sessions with himself every day, examining his conscience. When I met him casually one day, he embarked without warning on one of these sessions. After half an hour there was no sign of diminution, so I said to him (shock tactic), 'I don't believe you have any conscience at all. If you had a conscience you would not have to examine it, it would examine you!' Did he like that? No he did not.

A week later I met him again, and I could see him carefully stepping around the question of conscience: clearly he expected nothing from me in that quarter. Instead he spoke at length on the importance of defending the truth. All his sessions were monologues, I noticed, so hit-and-run was the only way to cope with him. 'We don't need to defend the truth,' I said to him, 'the truth defends us!' This was so like the previous week's hit-and-run that he has studiously avoided me ever since. Well, at least, that gives him something else to study besides himself. And listening to his monologues was only encouraging him.

It is not your conscience you should examine, but your life. Why the reflexive twist? Why turn it in? Why make it a sitting duck for the ego? And in what spirit do you examine? Do you wear a wig and gown as you sit in judgment? Do you examine in order to absolve or condemn, or do you examine in order to find out what is happening, to understand?

I think we should try to understand. It is the truth that sets us free. Conscience is not a private inner world sufficient to itself, monologuing ceaselessly; it is a search for the truth, wherever the truth is to be found, inside or outside. Your life has an inner and an outer side to it, and you look at both together, because you are one whole person, not two halves. The trouble with conscience as an inner self-sufficient world is that it is very likely to set itself up against everything external: 'my conscience tells me' – as if your conscience couldn't be dead wrong. You are as likely to make a mistake in conscience as in any other area of your life, and probably more so.

Which brings me back to the conscience-man who talked at such length about defending the truth. The first thing we have to say about the truth is not that we have to defend it but that we have to stand in it. If I try to defend the truth without loving it, wanting to know it more and more profoundly, submitting myself to it, being sensitive to every nuance of it, I will do it more harm than good. 'What is truth?' asked Pilate, and Jesus did not answer by starting up an argument, but by standing in the truth. More lives are changed by a humble manifestation of the truth than by all the arguments that have ever been used to knock out an opponent. The truth will defend me if I stand in it. Lies stand up only for a short time; then they fall, and those who have stood in them will fall with them. There is no better camouflage for a lie than much talk about the truth, and the ego, the fundamental lie, loves the role of defender of the truth, just as it loves to masquerade as conscience.

The Lord said, 'I am the way, the truth and the life.' It is a useful experiment to put his name in place of the word 'truth' when you are trying to see what makes sense. So, conscience is a search for Christ. And Christ will set you free. I wonder if the conscience-man is still defending Christ: reversing the roles, saving the Saviour. It is like the case of the bishop who concluded his night prayer with, 'Good night, Jesus!' And Jesus replied, 'Good night, my Lord!'

Patterns

Imagine a spillage of water on a sloped surface. The water trickles down, making an irregular path as it goes. Later on, some more water is spilt, and you see how unhesitatingly in runs in the path that was made before. It could make a new path for itself, but since there is no need to do so, it doesn't. It follows the easiest route; it is 'fluent' in the literal sense of the word: it flows.

Human experience seems to be like that. It could make new paths for itself every day, but usually it doesn't bother to do so. In times of crisis, or in very creative moments, we could break out into new paths; but we usually just follow the routes we have been following all our lives. So our normal experience has a kind of 'fluency' about it: it flows along old paths. Those paths were first laid down in childhood. We are not limited to those early paths, but out of force of habit (and laziness and fear and lack of imagination) we act as if we were bound by them.

How did you get by as a child? How did you stay out of trouble while getting what you wanted? By becoming invisible? If so, then the chances are that you are still doing that, that you are comfortable at the edge of a group, not at the centre, and you may notice that people often cut across your conversation. Or was it by shouting louder? If you were let get away with that, then you probably now have a commanding voice and you use it to shout people down and bulldoze their objections. Or was it by being very sweet and charming? You still are, probably.... There must be many other ways too of getting by. We saw very early in life that some tricks worked and others did not; so we chose the most successful one. Small children sometimes understand their parents better than their parents understand them. They have perfect cover: everyone thinks they understand nothing! When we were children, our chosen method served us well, so we didn't need to change it. But after some years it had become so much part of our personality that to change it even for a moment would be like walking naked down the street.

A useful key to your personality, then, is the discovery of your principal childhood technique. We are being persuaded on all sides that human personality is the deepest mystery, but in fact, for the most part, it is frighteningly repetitive and boring. Try this ten-second experiment (and please do no exceed the time-limit!): look at yourself and at others as monstrously overgrown babies and toddlers, see the trick that has become second nature, and ask yourself: Do I really think God created that?

My being is deeper than my personality. God creates my being. I myself, in collusion with parents and others who didn't always see through me, created my personality. Which of these do I bring to God when I pray? Some few tricks of personality? No, these fool no one, not even myself. What do I bring? Nothing. Or perhaps I can say: my being. Before God, I am always walking naked down the street. Surely, you say, in addition to my being, I bring my thoughts and my feelings? Well, perhaps I can bring a few of those, if they are not too fluent.

Imitation

Imagine a poet awake all night, watching and waiting for the right words to come. Hour after hour he or she sits or paces up and down, now in high spirits, now in low, jubilant at times, or moaning, now very quiet and now agitated, biting the end of a pencil or filling the waste-paper basket with crumpled paper.... Suddenly the words are there, shining in the mind and on the page. How was it done? Is success the result of effort? Could I do it if I put in the work? If I spent a night imitating that poet – pacing up and down, sighing so many times a minute, biting a certain number of pencils and filling a basket, etc. – would I also produce a poem in the small hours? No. Work will not do it. But neither will leisure. At another time those or better words might have come without effort or pain, yet if the poet were to rely on such moments of grace and refuse to work and suffer, those moments would probably never come. Sweat and tears are necessary, yet poetry is the result of inspiration, not of sweat and tears.

In the place of poets put saints. Now what happens? All the pious people of the world begin to imitate them: the things they did and said, the feelings they are supposed to have had, sometimes even the way they dressed. But, you say, didn't St Paul write, 'I urge you … be imitators of me' (1 Corinthians 4:16)? Yes, and you could mention three other passages in which he said the same thing. But he also wrote in Ephesians 5:1, 'Be imitators of God.' This is nearer to what Matthew reports of Jesus, who said, 'You must be perfect as your heavenly Father is perfect' (5:48). How are we to think about imitation in the spiritual life? I once heard an honest man say that all imitation is external and monkey-like. Is that the only honest view? Let's call a witness: Meister Eckhart of Hochheim.

He wrote, 'People may become anxious and distressed because the lives of our Lord Jesus Christ and of the saints were so harsh and laborious, and one may not be able to imitate them in this.… Take heed of how you ought to follow God. You ought to know and to take heed of what it is that God is requiring most of you; for not everyone is called to come along the same way to God, as St Paul says. It is not possible for everyone to live alike, for all to follow one single way of life, or for one person to adopt what another or everyone else is doing.… One ought indeed to imitate our Lord, but still not in everything he did.'

This seems sensible advice. We are not to imitate anyone slavishly, not even Christ; we are to imitate 'spiritually' and 'with our reason,' he said further on. If we imitate slavishly we are slaves. Our Father's house is not a place of slavery, nor is it a place of neglect; it is a house of love. We are not imprisoned, nor are we left to our own devices. We have freedom to be who we are, yet we are never abandoned. Eckhart catches the balance of it perfectly: 'Each of us ought to imitate him in our own way.' It may sound like a contradiction: if it is imitation it is not our own way, and if it is our own way it is not imitation. But by instinct we know what he means.

A poet's imagination finds body in words; a Christian is inspired by the Holy Spirit to give body to the Word of God. The cases are not entirely different. The Christian life is hard work, and yet it is all grace. External imitation may show desire and good will (or insecurity and fear), but inspiration is 'spiritual' and 'with our reason.'

Multiply illustrations of this if you will. Athletes put themselves through physical regimes that make the lives of Carthusian monks look soft and self-indulgent. This is because they are heart and soul in love with their game. Love urges you to tremendous effort, but no amount of effort can urge you to tremendous love, nor even to mediocre love. We whittle down the truth of this by repeating that love is a decision; the intention is to say that work can get you there. In the absence of deep understanding and an inner spirit of love, such sacrificial love breeds guilt and resentment.

The question is: how do we learn to love? Where do we start? Certainly not from the ego. The ego knows nothing about love: it knows only about looking good and taking credit for everything; it corrupts love, putting a lie where the truth should be. So how do we learn to love? Where do we start? It is a very difficult question, and it is not surprising that in the absence of clarity we start with the most obvious side of it, the works of love. All the better then, we think, if we can find a rule-book that tells us how to proceed. In this way, from time immemorial, religion has tended to turn into rules of behaviour.

How does a Christian learn to love God? The traditional

answer, rather disappointing for the ego, is that we don't really! It is 'infused', it is a gift; you just have to be in the right place at the right time and it is yours. The place is the Church, the Christian community; the time is now, the time of the new covenant. Instead of trying to learn to love, we should try to understand how we manage to unlearn it! The ego would like to be responsible for a big love-project, but there is nothing here for the ego. The ego is a perfect monkey; and monkeys are no poets, nor great lovers, nor do they have any scrap of faith.

Just watch with careful attention the way you live, the way you act, the way you react, the contents of your mind when you are with people, when you are alone, when you are daydreaming. Just watch and try to understand. There are no rules for doing this.

On the other hand

'On the one hand,' he said, 'I think I should go ahead, but on the other hand.... ' I noticed that this was how he approached everything: by hesitating, thinking thoughts that cancelled one another out, and doing nothing in the end. I remember seeing someone like him being interviewed, and after some time the interviewer asked in frustration, 'But if you had only one hand, what would you say?'

You have two hands, yes, but they are different, are they not? Open them before you, and you see that they are two quite different models: the thumb, for example, is on the left side of one of them and on the right of the other. They are not equal, they are not designed to do two equal and separate jobs, but one. They are designed to co-operate with each other; they are two, but they are a little community of one; they are the instruments of one brain. So, 'on the one hand and on the other hand' is evidence of a brain that cannot get itself together. I was once speaking with a man who lost count of his points of view, and had he totted up he would have found that he had laid claim to three or four hands! I knew another who always said 'On the one hand ... and on the other,' but then within minutes he always said, 'I think.... ' There is a difference between vacillating and balancing.

The difference between thinking and doing is that you can think a thousand things together, even incompatible things, but you can usually do only one at a time. This transition from the profusion of possibilities to the poverty of a single deed is too much for some. 'On the one side,' he had been saying, 'and on the other ... ' (perhaps someone had teased him about hands and now he said sides). We three had been pacing around near Trajan's column for more than an hour, and he had not reached a single conclusion. When faced with a fact, his trick was to divide his mind in two and pass it by on both sides. 'Why don't you try and walk around that column on both sides at once?' said the other person, suddenly abandoning his patience. But it was futile; he looked seriously at the column as if to see whether it could be done. We got nowhere that afternoon, nor at any other time. He is still thinking and considering and looking at both sides ... and doing nothing.

To finish considering and to begin to do one thing – to choose one way – seems like poverty. We wonder if we are missing something. This is especially true of us today when countless alternatives to everything we have ever thought and said and done are paraded before us. We can envisage different lives, and this is one of the ways in which we are different from the animals; but when the very variety of possibilities prevents us from doing any one thing, or doing it right, we have to begin to make choices.

'You must always do one thing, you cannot do everything ...' said Meister Eckhart. 'It must always be one thing, and in that one, you should find everything. For if you wanted to do everything, this and that, dropping your way for another's way, which you liked better, truly that would make for great instability.... Choose a good way and keep to it, introducing all good ways into it and bearing in mind that it comes from God, instead of starting one thing today and something else tomorrow. You need not worry that you are missing anything. For with God one can miss nothing. With God you can no more miss anything than God can miss anything. So, take one way from God, and embody in it all good things.'

The fact that Eckhart had to say this is proof that the young men he was speaking to on that occasion, in the fourteenth century, were capable of being quite as dopey as the person of my acquaintance. Occasionally thought can be revolutionary, but mostly it is at the service of the ego, maintaining everything just as it was before, out of fear, allowing nothing to happen, good or bad.

The divine economy

When I was ten I had a religious conversion. I became keenly interested in indulgenced prayers. I saw that the price range was very wide. Some, the plenary indulgences, were like blank cheques; it almost made one dizzy to think about them. Then there was the largest denomination: seven years and seven quarantines. The quarantines were a small mystery; they were like a special offer package; I didn't know whether I wanted them or not, but the offer seemed generous anyway. Then there were lesser and lesser denomination notes till you got to the coins: three hundred days, a hundred days and even fifty days (these last were like halfpennies). I built up my account ravenously, specialising in the bigger notes. Somehow, for all their great value, plenary indulgences never attracted me very much. What does one plenary indulgence add to another, since each one is plenary? You cannot collect them, unless of course you collect them for other people, like the Souls in Purgatory; but I wasn't much interested in boosting their profits; young businessmen have to concentrate on their own careers. Sometimes the day's takings came close to two thousand years and several hundred quarantines. In big numbers the quarantines became annoying if anything. I couldn't add them into the other column, since I didn't know what they were worth; and if I just gave them a value it would introduce a note of subjectivity into all my calculations; no business person would ever do such a thing. So there they were, occupying a kind of mental space, not really useful for anything – unless the Holy Souls might be interested in them.... A short time after that I became interested in collecting conkers. They were so bright when they were new, like polished mahogany. But the old ones were good too, and what they lacked in freshness they made up for in numbers. So keen did I get on them that I lost track of my earlier business entirely, never even bothering to work out a full bank statement. The account is still there I suppose ... unless those Holy Souls....

The doctrine underlying indulgences is very liberating: we don't have to earn every penny ourselves; we are already rich; 'Christ, though he was rich, for your sake became poor, so that by his poverty you might become rich' (2 Corinthians 8:9). We don't need, then, to 'build up a spiritual life' (as the depressing phrase has it). There is nothing worse than a spiritually self-made man; there is always something ungenerous and competitive about him, he never becomes used to spiritual wealth, he keeps watching pennies all his life. But we are rich with the riches of Christ. We have inherited wealth and we are used to it. We are not the *nouveaux riches*, we don't have to be tight-fisted, we can live like our Father who doesn't pay by the hour (Matthew 20:1-16), and who 'makes the sun rise on the evil and on the good, and sends rain on the just and on the unjust' (Matthew 5:45), never enquiring whether they have earned it. The doctrine underlying indulgences is meant to wean us from the urge to be spiritually self-supporting. The danger begins when we begin to count. I have found that counting is always a danger sign in the spiritual life. It was the Pharisee in the front row who had all his figures ready: he fasted twice a week, he gave tithes (= 10%) of all he possessed....

The miserly collector is always ready to slip in and turn it all into a little business. In a child it seems innocent enough, or at any rate blatant enough to be curable, but we can easily retain it into adult life simply by hiding it better. Or at least, traces of it can remain in us: the greedy fingers are always there, and the voluminous pocket. The degeneration that overtakes the doctrine of indulgences is very like the degeneration of the cult of saints' relics. Both are ways of saying: I want a little piece just for myself. I have seen tourists chipping fragments off monuments and making off with them, and I think the urge in all cases is the same: it is the urge to collect. The ego is insecurity itself, and this painful feeling is somewhat alleviated by collecting. Even symbolic collecting will do. There is a squirrel in everyone (a whole jungle of animals if it comes to it!) The squirrel is the acquisitive one: collecting for little me. See how embarrassing it is when someone catches you at it! The tinier the meanness the worse it is, because you have thought smaller and stooped lower. Meanness in regard to anything is shameful in a Christian: that is not how we have been taught to live. The ego calls it by many names: frugality, economy, thrift; but it is still only meanness. Theologians used to speak about 'the divine economy', but they never meant to suggest that it was a penny-pinching economy. Instead it is an economy of superabundance: where there are basketfuls left over from the meal and where wine is measured in jars that hold thirty or forty gallons apiece.

Games

Life is often chaotic, but when you play a game you make everything clear: you take a little part of life and you decide very clear rules, time-limits and boundaries to it. Unlike life, the beginning and the end are both subject to your conscious decision, and so is everything in between: losses and gains are limited and clearly defined. It is a rest from the disturbing uncertainty of life itself, but it contains just enough of a simple kind of uncertainty to keep you interested. It is life in a smaller and more acceptable edition. We need to take the pressure off ourselves at times, to lower the stakes and to indulge in some innocent clarity. It rests the nerves.

Have you ever noticed that even very serious people are

inclined to run and shout and kick ball when they are at the seaside? Something there gives them permission to relax and be childlike again. Is it the sea? the wind? nature? Maybe. Or it may be no more than a convention: all agree that it is acceptable to behave like that when you are by the sea. There is a similar convention about pubs: people relax there because everyone agrees that you don't have to do anything useful in a pub. Since everyone else (except the barman) is doing nothing, you feel free to do nothing yourself; you are given permission to slake your righteous thirst without fear or favour.

Driving a car is not a game, but many men turn it into a game. I know a man who keeps up a running sports commentary as he drives; he describes everything that happens in the flow of traffic, and all his own moves, as strategies in a game of rugby. There are many also who turn money matters into a game, especially when speculation is part of it. And when you hear people talk about scoring points off one another, it sounds like boxing. It seems we can turn almost anything into a game, even our personal relationships.

Very well, why not take it to the end? Can we think of our relationship with God as a game? Why not? It is a beginning. A Rabbi said that the only reason suggested in the Scriptures why God created the world was: for fun. So why should not our relationship with God be expressed as a game?

What game, then? Hide-and-seek, I would suggest. Sometimes we hide and God seeks; sometime God hides and we seek. But if one gives up, the game is over. Sometimes God seems to be in hiding not just for five or ten minutes but for years; and we can discover that we have spent half a lifetime hiding from God. But we are assured that even if we hang back for years, God will not give up.

Someone suggested a variation on hide-and-seek. It is called 'Sardines'. When you find the person who is hiding, you don't shout and give the game away; you climb in, and the two of you hide together! After a while there are three of you, and four, and five. Then it becomes increasingly hard to suppress the giggling, which of course blows your cover, and eventually the whole crowd of you are sprawled around the place, laughing and pushing and shouting. Maybe that is how it will be at the end of time! Our departed friends have climbed in with God and are hiding from us, waiting, full of longing and excitement. God will be discovered, and we will all be discovered ... and astonished and happy at our discovery ... in the end!

Is that too optimistic for you, too good to be true? All right. Try snakes-and-ladders, then. Ladders are about climbing, pulling yourself up, improving your position. Climbing is hard, and it is all your own work. As a religion, this would be a DIY affair: be your own Saviour, and you won't have to pay or thank anybody. But since you are on your own, you will have to have eyes in the back of your head: there is no Providence to make good your mistakes, and there are dangers lurking everywhere. Reality cannot be trusted: there are snakes. When you meet a snake, your climbing is undone and you have to start again from far back, perhaps even from the beginning. The religious game of snakes-and-ladders produces some very depressing people, who teach you to observe yourself and log your progress; they teach you to count. This may provide you with a certain satisfaction at times, or a feeling of security, but what is remarkable is the absence of joy. Real joy is uncaused, it is something the ego cannot produce or control, it is from beyond, it is one of the fruits of the Spirit (Galatians 5:22). When Jesus speaks of the Father in Luke 15, joy is the theme (because it is all about losing and finding – hide-and-seek). God, he said, is like a shepherd who searches for the lost sheep, joyfully puts it on his shoulders and calls his friends and neighbours to tell them, 'Rejoice with me ... !' Or God is like the woman who found the lost money and did the same. Or like the father of the prodigal son, an old man who in his joy forgot his years and ran towards his son, and said to everybody, 'It is right to celebrate and rejoice!'

God plays hide-and-seek (or Sardines), and has joy over us. The ego's games, by contrast, are selfish and obsessive. One might have expected the German mystics to revel in dissecting and labelling the spiritual life, but never; Eckhart's vision is hide-and-seek. When you find people looking into themselves and trying to identify what stage of spirituality they are at, you can be excused for thinking of the numbers on a snakes-and-ladders board. The trademark of the ego is numbers.

Taking flight

Nothing defines us so well as the kind of holiday we choose for ourselves. It is by nature something free, and it shows what we make of our freedom when left to ourselves. I want to say that we take many holidays – not just at Christmas and in the summer – and they all have the power to show us things of great significance about ourselves.

If by a holiday I mean a time to 'flop out', then I am taking a holiday every time I reward myself with a coffee or a smoke or by putting my feet on the table, or by going to the pub. This defines the rest of my life as tension, from which I need release every so often. Tension (at least tension of the wrong kind) means conflict, absence of harmony. So I am saying: my life constrains me, it is a heavy imposition, an alien burden laid upon me; and I need to withdraw from it as often as I can, to make time for me. In other words, my life is not my own; only the moments when I flop out from it are mine. And the more disciplined my life requires me to be, the more often and the further I will flop.

Such a terrible alienation: to think that my life is not my own! The compensations for such a feeling could never be enough. What am I to do? Withdraw into a permanent state of flop-out? Some do this, but it is much more terrible than any other way. I know that the only way is to give up trying to escape from my life, to turn right around and go more deeply into it. Bring your chest up to it, gently, I say to myself, and keep going.

A young married man came for help to a Vietnamese Zen Master. His problem was the combined pressures of work and family life. He knew he should spend as much time as possible with his wife and young son, but precisely at that time his job was requiring his soul of him. He was beginning to lose his competitive edge at work, and at the same time (and for that very reason) he was not enjoying his time with his wife and son: he was losing both ways. This was an exhausting experience, and therefore he needed time just for himself, to gather his strength. It was a double-bind, or a triple. Everything he did was a betrayal of everything else that he had to do, and yet he could not leave any of them. In trying to do the best for everyone he was succeeding only in doing the worst. It had come to a head: 'I have no time for myself!' he said.

You have divided your life into three parts, said the Zen Master: your work, your family and yourself. But this makes no sense. The time you spend with your wife, is it not your time too? Is it not for you as much as it is for her? The time you spend playing with your son, is it not your time as much as his? You have been dividing yourself, and that is the origin of the trouble. You are dividing yourself from what you do. You are putting yourself outside your life, as if it were a task you had to do. But our life is a communion, not a task. If it were a task, you would have to ask: who is the person who is performing this task, and where is he? Let me tell you: he is the ego, a hungry ghost, disconnected from everything and trying to control everything from the outside. Your life includes many tasks, but it is not itself a task; it is a communion. Your time with your wife is your time; your time with your son is your time. If you learn this profoundly you may even come to see that the time you spend working is also your time. In the end you will see that your whole life is yours! Learn this as quickly as you can, because it is only when your life is yours that you can give it to others.

The biggest problem in western societies, he said, is this sense of alienation, this sense of being an outsider to one's own life. We have become alienated spooks, hard lonely creatures who control (or try to control) everything and cannot be part of anything. We need to learn communion with others and with our own work. We need to learn how to lose ourselves in a good way. If we don't learn this, we will spend our lives compensating ourselves by losing ourselves in a bad way: by getting drunk, by getting sloppy and irresponsible about everything, by 'flopping out'. Our experience, he concluded, is able to teach us much more than we know. We just have to go into it, not out of it. Don't flop out, don't take flight; that is the ego's solution. Look into it with careful attention; then go into it, and you will experience communion.

The outsider

I remember him still, though it must be thirty years since we met – if we ever met. He was not a person you could ever meet in the ordinary way; instead, he studied you as an entomologist might study a revolting insect, but with far less feeling. He was very intelligent but unfriendly and friendless. He was an outsider. I don't know what became of him, but at eighteen he had already assembled all the ingredients for an unhappy life.

The outsider, the observer, the critic: a race of people who are given absolute authority in our age. Swift called them 'the tribes of Answerers, Considerers, Observers, Reflectors, Detectors, Remarkers.' What would he call them were he alive today? Journalists and literary and art critics rule far beyond their constituencies. The outsider probably found a home among them, in the measure of the possible.

But we should not talk about 'them', as if we ourselves were not part of it. If we read newspapers or watch television we are part of it. And we do. I do. We are talking about ourselves and our world. It is not only strange recluses who peep out at the world from behind the curtain; their habit is only an exaggeration of a common human one: curiosity. Every valley is the valley of the squinting windows. 'The human mind … loves to lie concealed,' wrote St Augustine in the fifth century, 'yet it wishes that nothing should be concealed from it.' The urge to hide suggests that there may be a lie lurking somewhere.

The 'ego' is the false self. I don't mean only the self that tells the odd fib to fool other people; I mean the self that fools itself. It is not my real self (of which I may indeed have little or no knowledge), but my idea of myself, my self-image. It is the encrustation of millions of experiences, big and small, throughout my life – all of course from the past. This encrustation prevents new experiences from touching me, unless they confirm what I already think I am. Simone Weil spoke of the 'arsenal of lies' that the ego throws up to defend itself. It is extremely insecure, being false, so it takes whatever means it can to protect and preserve itself. All new experiences are looked at in a sidelong way; I have to be cautious, I tell myself, because the new is always a threat to the security of the old. ('The past, at least, is secure,' said some politician, busily making a mess of the present.) The ego is always old, and the more I flee from present experience the more I strengthen that same ego and come to live from it.

If we are to relate to one another (or indeed to anything) in the present, we have to be new people every moment. We need openness, freedom from our own past, freedom from the need to label one another; in a word, we need to learn complete simplicity and humility. Egos can do an imitation of these, but there is always a lie in it. Nor can two egos ever really meet. Instead they watch one another; they observe from just out of reach. Or …

Or they merge. This merging is called 'falling in love'. 'I love you', coming from an egocentric person, means, 'Come into my territory, identify yourself with me, give me pleasure and lifelong emotional satisfaction, exist on my terms, be mine. But don't challenge my self-image; if you do I will leave you and look for someone else who will do all this for me.' Such persons, though they sometimes imagine themselves deeply in love, are outsiders still: they are unrelated and alone in the world.

We live in a brutal world where people kill and exploit one another as a matter of course. We are part of it; we may even watch it on TV as news entertainment (in many instances news programmes are designed in that format). There is an absolute need to stop being part of that violence and exploitation. If we are not part of the solution, it is said, we are part of the problem. But our wise people have little of value to say to us. Most western philosophies fail to challenge the ego; instead, for the most part, they trap it even more securely in itself. (Or when they challenge it, they plunge into various forms of nihilism, leaving nothing standing.) Why, because they are that very ego itself philosophising. With few exceptions, the so-called revolutionary new approaches produce only more of what we are used to. And despite the Gospel, much of theology simply follows suit, thinking this the most up-to-date thing it could do. The Reflectors, Detectors, Remarkers are rife in theology, because so much theology arises out of academic rather than religious experience.

Nothing less than the mind and heart of Christ will heal the outsider in us all.

FIVE

Meditation: Emptiness Is Depth

Monastery

Mount St Benedict, Tunapuna, Trinidad, West Indies: an
address tells you little or nothing, nothing of the spirit of a place.
But if your impression was that Trinidad was all Carnival swirl,
you have at least learnt from the address that there are monasteries there too. In fact, at that address you find two of them, an
old disused one and a new.

The old monastery was made of wattle and daub (clay and
wattles, to you). It was a very little monastery, with many small
windows, doorways, corners, passages, steps up and down. It
scarcely looked like a planned building at all, it was more like a
thing of nature that happened to sprout on that spot. The most
whimsical thing about it was a passage that ran right through the
middle, lengthways, and out both ends without a door. They
told me the reason. When monks first came there, long ago, the
terrain was extremely rough and there was only one place to
build the monastery: right on the path that led up the mountain.
This they did, but they allowed the path to be. They loaded a
donkey with two bales of hay and measured from side to side:
that became the width of the corridor!

The world was able to pass through the monastery. Today
there is a new monastery nearby, and the world still passes
through it, though not in the literal way of the old monastery.
Not only Christians of every kind come there looking for peace
and wisdom – Baptists, Pentecostalists as much as Catholics –
but even Hindus, Buddhists and Muslims.

The world must be able to pass through your monastery –

through your contemplative centre, your heart, your heart of prayer; otherwise that centre is only an escape to nowhere. A monastery with a thoroughfare, a heart pierced by the world: contemplation in some way resembles death. You are not insulated in the hard shell of your ego; you are accessible, you are vulnerable, you are pierced. At the heart of contemplation you meet the infinite God who lays you open, and not a tiny localised god who protects you. And you are not settling, in contemplation, for a tiny patch of world; your heart is expanding to embrace it in its entirety, more than if you were superficially bound into its affairs.

The life of a monk seems quite exceptional, different in every way from the life of an ordinary lay Christian. Yet it is right to remember that monks, typically, are laymen; and nuns are laywomen. Anthony of the Desert, the founder of monasticism, was and always remained a layman. When more and more monks became priests, their abbots began to resemble bishops, with mitre and crozier. But monasticism, at heart, is a lay movement. What monks do, then, has something to say to every Christian. They make visible the contemplative side of all Christian life. They live in this world, not in the skies. Therefore we cannot put them in a separate category or make them our substitutes; they are there to recall us to the contemplative side of our faith. If some of us need to pass sometimes through their monasteries, it is in order to pass through our own heart, our contemplative centre.

The Abbot of Mount St Benedict was a magnificent specimen of humanity: six foot four, with a straight back, a tremendous calm and a beard that swept down from the heights like the grace of God. In his white habit he fitted one's idea of an Old Testament prophet. Since I was a guest in the monastery I was placed beside him in choir. As we all bowed low at the 'Glory be to the Father' I glanced to the side and saw that he was wearing ... a pair of runners!

Sit up !

Whatever is in your mind and emotions becomes incarnated in your body; you may conceal it for a minute or for half a lifetime, but sooner or later it will out. When Lincoln was choosing his cabinet and a certain name was suggested, he said: 'No ... I don't like his face!' 'But he is not responsible for his face,' said someone. 'After the age of forty,' replied Lincoln, 'everyone is responsible for his face!'

You, reader, if you are a shy person, ill at ease with most people and terrified of displeasing anybody, I have something to say to you. Come here. Sit down. Now sit up! Stop smiling! You are overdoing it, like a dog wagging its tail and wagging its hindquarters with it. Relax! Take a few deep breaths.

Now stand up! Oh look how you lean forward, as if to go more than half-way to meet people! Then in order to keep your balance you have to go slack at the knees. We have to rebuild you from the ground up! Stand squarely on the floor, feet apart, balanced: those two small patches of ground belong to you while you are standing on them; no one else can stand there; they are your claim on existence. Seeing that God allows you to exist, you have a right to be here. To support your top half as it leans forward you have had to bring forward your hips. Put them back in their place! Now see how your spine makes its natural S-shaped curve, and your shoulders can come back into a strong dignified position, without the least strain. Now put your head back on your body! It has been lolling forward, to compensate for the crookedness below it. It hardly seems part of your body at all; is it any wonder you always have a pain in your neck? To put your head right, push in your chin a little. Now your head is in continuity with the body; it is the flowering of your spinal column, rather than a heavy object hanging at the top of it. This is the way you were designed; the other was your own idea. You look better. You are now a fine cut of a man. You are a graceful lady. You have presence. Your posture foretells the kind of death you are going to have – a collapse or a consummation.

'The body must retain its own dignity,' said Tauler. The Word was made flesh; everything, for a Christian, tends to become flesh, to take on body. Good thoughts are meant to flower into good deeds. Prayer is not a merely mental or spiritual exercise; it is from our whole being, body and soul. 'Christian, know your dignity!' should have effects like the ones I just described.

Now I will describe a way of breathing that will help you. The very word 'spirit' comes from *spirare* and means 'to breathe', which suggests a connection between breathing and the spiritual life. God formed Adam from the dust of the earth, 'and breathed into his nostrils the breath of life' (Genesis 2:7). Our breath is God's life in us.

Still standing in your corrected posture, breathe in. As you do, imagine that the breath is rising like a life-force through your spine, and that your whole body is blossoming into its full shape; you have an inner vigour that reaches all the way through your body and up into your head. Then imagine that it turns there and descends through your chest. Pause, then breathe again, up ... and down.

Do you sit or kneel down to pray or meditate every day? Tomorrow morning sit on a meditation stool or a hard chair, in a quiet place (soft chairs don't support your body, they allow you to slump). Hold your body upright, without strain; don't lean against the back of the chair. Breathe, in the way I described. As you breathe in, receive the gift of God's life (in particular the virtue of fortitude, one of the seven gifts of the Spirit), then downwards in fruitfulness for the world, giving everything away, as in a beautiful death. Or imagine that your being is like a tree (a tree has excellent posture!), with the sap of life rising through it, then reaching down its arms, its branches, weighed with fruit. Once you get the feel of meditation you will not need any images to describe it, nor any instructions on how to do it. There is no need to talk, unless you particularly want to; we are meant to be God's familiars. You are praying, or meditating (it hardly matters what you call it).

Later in the day you will often find your old posture and attitude returning ('I don't want to be exposed to these people, I want to run away ... '), if this is the kind of person you are. Breathe up and down two or three times. The strength of your meditation will return to you.

Of course you may not be the sagging type at all; you may be as proud and perpendicular as a prince. If so, I must tell you not to forget to breathe out!

But no matter how you express your north-south polarity, the enduring factors are the same: you stand between heaven and earth, like all of us. Earth is gravity and stability, heaven is an open space into which you raise your head and shoulders, your whole body. A perfect balance of these is perfect dignity.

Shoes off

In *An Evil Cradling*, in which Brian Keenan vividly described his kidnapping and imprisonment in Beirut by Islamic fundamentalists, there is a passage where he speaks of a fearful attachment to his shoes. If these were taken away from him, he felt, he would surely never see freedom again. When you have no shoes you are going nowhere. In some religious traditions the shoes are always removed before meditation, and perhaps for a similar reason: to meditate is to stop moving.

To meditate is to stop moving, to stop running away. It is to 'imprison' oneself in a discipline of meditation and to make oneself vulnerable. Jesus was fastened hand and foot to the cross: this meant that he could do nothing and go nowhere. In some icons he is called the *Pantokrator*, the Ruler of all; but in the supreme moment of his life he could not rule even his own limbs. Clearly the word 'freedom' is one of those deep but highly ambiguous words.

If you are in prison you are unfree in a physical sense, but spiritually and mentally you may be very free: much more so than any of your warders, perhaps. If you are out of prison you are free in a physical sense, but spiritually and mentally you may be deeply enslaved. Walking around, apparently in freedom, are millions of people who are securely imprisoned in themselves: through addictions of all sorts, through fear of ever being alone and unoccupied for more than a little while, through mental or physical laziness, through enslavement to passions and evil habits....

The deepest enslavement is to oneself. Personal freedom is a personal conquest, wise men and women tell us: high talk has nothing to do with it; much of what is trumpeted about freedom is only a rattling of chains. We inflame one another about external freedom because we are all equally embarrassed by our own spiritual and mental slavishness. A real conquest of freedom is an urgent matter for every person. If you are not free of yourself, we are told, you are not free at all. But if you are free of yourself, then nothing can imprison you.

Meditation is a conquest of inner freedom. You 'imprison' yourself in a practice of meditation in order to be deeply free of yourself. When I say 'imprison' I mean to say: hold yourself to the practice and do not let it depend on whims of the moment. Nothing is ever achieved by stopping and starting; you are up against the constant urge to enslave yourself in different ways, and so your effort has to be a constant one. Choose a time and place where you will meditate every day, and make it an invariable practice. Place an icon there, if you wish, and light a candle. Use whatever helps you. That place deserves honour, for it is going to become the anchorage of your life.

Take off your shoes! Begin by remembering the Lord's presence and asking for help. Remember the priceless gift of time that is given to you moment by moment. Be aware also of the constant urge there is to 'push' time past you: to overrun the present moment in order to make something happen.... Be aware of that restlessness. I don't say, Control it! (You would begin to do that with the very same restlessness.) Instead, be simply aware of it; that's enough. Anything else that may happen will happen of itself. It is a matter of getting down (on your knees, so to speak) to look at time in the closest possible way:

looking at the texture of it, knowing the feel of it, liking it, and not wishing to push it past you. Enter each moment as if it were an eternity. You are not going anywhere, you are not trying to make anything happen, you are simply sitting still and watching time closely as it passes. Time is a priceless gift of God; the least we can do is look closely at it. If a feeling of boredom assails you, look at it! Look at everything that arises within you. Just look, don't judge. And don't try to hurry anything up, or to slow anything down. If you can stay in that 'place', you have gone down below the storms of restlessness and all desire, the whirl-winds of addiction and compulsion, the disquiet that fear of being unoccupied causes in you. Only when viewed from that place can your thoughts and actions be really understood. That is the place where freedom is born.

Anchor

'Oh,' people say, 'if only I had a spiritual director to talk to! I get the most fearful ideas, and I am in a dreadful state!' This was Tauler, quoting what had been said to him, no doubt, many times. He was the most fatherly of the Rhineland mystics, and this is what he said in reply: 'My dear child, I know a lot about the ideas the devil can put in our minds, and my advice is this: what the devil puts in your mind, you put out again; be at peace and turn your heart to God. Pay no attention to such ideas ... just let them pass out of your mind.... Lay the burden of your cares on God, anchor yourself in God. When sailors are in danger and think they are going to run aground on the rocks, they throw their anchor overboard and it sinks to the bottom of the Rhine, and that saves them. We should do the same ... throw our anchor overboard, the anchor of perfect trust and hope in God. Never mind about the oars and the rudder, the anchor is all you need. And this is what you must do in every distress of soul or body.'

This kind of fatherly, or grandfatherly, advice is never out of date. We will always need that kind of advice, because there are so many who give us the opposite kind when we have a problem. 'What are you doing about it?' they demand. This 'what are you doing about it?' assumes that we are doing nothing, and presumes to urge us to do something; but when you think about it, isn't it much more likely, in an age of activism like ours, that we are doing too much? – too much, and possibly the wrong things. Frenzy doesn't have to look like frenzy: if I don't know what to do in some situation, and I do just anything for the sake of being busy, that is a kind of frenzy. It is like a wheel that is spinning with great momentum in the wrong direction; it has to stop before it can begin to go right. Or as Eckhart put it, speaking of people who strive in the wrong way: 'They go around like someone who has lost his way; the further he goes, the more he is lost.' How wise to tell us just to drop anchor for a while!

Meditation is about dropping anchor. You just stop your activity. This sounds very simple, but it is not as simple as it sounds. It is when you slow down or stop that you become aware of the restlessness that normally drives you. The mind and imagination wander aimlessly, the hands fidget, muscles here or there in the body are tensed up. All this was hidden before in the rush of action, but now it is plainly visible. Then you are tempted to give up meditation immediately: 'I'm no good at this!' No. Stay. Next you may try to quell that restlessness, but out of the same restless urge! It doesn't work; activism cannot cure activism. Instead, just wait! Allow the whole system to come slowly to rest. It will do this if you don't keep stirring it up. Whatever continues to arise in your mind, just watch and don't feed it. Gradually, over the shoulder, so to speak, of all these distractions you glimpse or sense a great calm, the background to everything. We can have a sense of God's presence in any and every part of our life, but it is very important to find God also in this 'soil', this deep calm humble place: for it is here that all our thoughts and actions and feelings have their roots.

I remember, at a meditation retreat, a man who was very unhappy with all that sitting in silence. 'Why don't you give us something we can think about?' he said, 'something from the

Scriptures, like "Be still and know that I am God"?' There we were, for hours every day, being still and trying to know that God was God, doing what the Scriptures told us to do; but he wanted to talk about it! – to talk about silence! He would have sung about it too, probably, given encouragement.

Once upon a time there were four monks who decided to make a silent retreat. After two days the silence bore too heavily on one of them and he went and spoke to one of the others. But the other replied, 'Don't you remember, Brother, that we vowed to be silent during this retreat?' In replying thus, of course, he himself had broken the silence! Meanwhile the third monk was passing by and spoke sternly to the two. 'Silence, you two!' he said. That made three who had now broken the silence. The fourth monk, passing in the distance, saw them and said triumphantly, 'I'm the only one who hasn't broken the silence!'

To be silent is to die a little. Yes, there are many people – even monks – who feel that they exist only if they are talking. What those monks in the story needed was four anchors. One each. 'Fearing that we might run on the rocks, they let out four anchors from the stern, and prayed for day to come' (Acts 27:29).

On being silent

Before you speak a word you are its master; after you speak it you are its slave. We know this saying but we don't know it at the very moment we need to know it! 'I could have bitten my tongue off,' we say. Without a habit of being silent sometimes, we will surely stumble often into speech when we should have remained silent.

A habit of silence: this means a frequent choice of silence over words. Why should that be a good thing? Because if there is no silence, words have no background, and therefore they lose their power. With no background the foreground is all clutter, like an oriental bazaar; nothing stands out because everything stands out equally. The surrounding air is filled with a turbulence of words. But one's own head is likewise filled, and this is the more serious matter.

What if words were visible? We put signs of them on paper, yes, but I don't mean that. What if they were visible in the air, like things or patterns? They would certainly make a moving, sometimes a dizzying, display. Even when you think you are making a regular pattern, as on a rug or a carpet, others may see your meaning back to front. Don Quixote pronounced translations to be 'like viewing Flemish tapestries from the wrong side,' but even an ordinary conversation in one's own language can be like that. What a crazy entanglement of threads and wisps of speech, with gaps everywhere, all irregular, and with muddles of colour large and small ...! Sometimes a pattern begins to appear, but mostly there is a bustling in one direction and then in another; and the whole is hung with superfluous frills and flounces, fringes and trimmings, tassels and knots. What is it for? Not for keeping. Mostly it passes immediately into oblivion, meant for no other purpose than to kill time. Yet it often attains to the level of an art. Against all appearances, this fantastic creation is a perfect instrument for our purposes. And so, when our purpose is to waste time it fulfils that purpose perfectly.

Speech is often a release of nervous energy, a kind of earthing of tension. And so nothing builds up inside. I think we should let things grow inside us: let them germinate in darkness and give them plenty of time. In the face of all great things we need to be silent. In the face of death: silence. A Zimbabwean friend told me that in her country when you visit a bereaved family you do *kubata maoko*, which is, to hold hands in silence. You cannot do it by post or over the phone; you are there in person. You offer your presence, not your words of comfort (it is easy for you to feel comfortable). How much more sensible than the embarrassed mutterings we go on with! We never know what to say (what can we say?), so we mutter and look embarrassed; or we say, 'What can I say?' It might be a good idea to say nothing. In many other situations, likewise, how strong and good silence could be!

Even before small things: silence. When you see shrubs and flowers do you have to be able to name them? Many people believe that they don't know a plant unless they know its name, and conversely that if they know its name they know enough about the plant. Can you look up at the night sky without quoting some figures from astronomy or reciting a line of some poem? Young children can be our teachers here: see how they can become absorbed in things, see how silent they can be, see how they just look.

> Children are dumb to say how hot the day is,
> How hot the scent is of the summer rose,
> How dreadful the black wastes of evening sky,
> How dreadful the tall soldiers drumming by.
>
> But we have speech, to chill the angry day,
> And speech, to dull the rose's cruel scent.
> We spell away the overhanging night,
> We spell away the soldiers and the fright. (Robert Graves)

Three pious sheep

Never before had I met a sheep with a name, but on that day I met three of them. It was in Manila, a city of about twelve million people (more, some say, but no one seems to know for sure). It was all the more surprising, then, to find sheep there with names. These sheep were living in a convent. They had entered there as lambs and grown to adulthood within its walls. No, they were not meant for the pot – far from it, they had almost become members of the community, and I will tell you the reason.

The Scriptures are full of references to sheep, because Palestine was a world in which sheep figured very largely. In the book of Genesis there are references to sheep-shearing. A shepherd would go to great trouble to find a lost sheep, he would carry an injured lamb or sheep in his arms, and might even die in defence of his flock. The shepherd's care for the sheep became an image of God's care for people, and a sinner was 'a lost sheep'. Jesus called himself a shepherd. In Christian language the word 'pastoral' is commonplace: it comes from the Latin word *pastor*, which means 'shepherd'. There is the prophet Nathan's parable of the poor man who had only 'one little ewe lamb.' 'He brought it up, and it grew up with him and with his children; it used to eat of his morsel, and drink from his cup, and lie in his bosom, and it was like a daughter to him' (2 Sam 12:3). However, Nathan did not give that little ewe a name (though the reference was to be quite clear later on). Which brings me back to the sheep in the Manila convent.

Those three sheep did have names (which I will not tell you yet). Like the sheep in Nathan's parable, they used to wander around the house, beg at table (they had a partiality for rice) and feel quite at home at all times. Why were they there? They were there because the novice mistress was aware that none of her novices had ever seen a sheep in her life, though they were reading about them every day in the Scriptures. She had a good instinct: she wanted to make things visible, tangible, material; every word should eventually become flesh in one way or another. So far so good. But the opposite instinct began to work almost immediately: the instinct to turn everything into words. It showed in the names she gave the sheep. I will now reveal those names. They were: Humility, Purity and Prayer.

'Come out of there, Humility!' 'Purity, go away please!' Talking to those sheep made you feel silly. They may have felt a bit silly themselves, because they began to develop traits that were in all cases the exact opposite of their names. Humility head-butted the prioress, Prayer made mistakes in the chapel, and Purity fell in love with Humility. Nature (or something) takes its revenge when you get silly with it.

How would you like to be known yourself? As Ambition? Or perhaps Pride, or Temperance? We would get used to it, up to a point. We are already used to it in small doses: we don't think it strange that a girl should be called Joy, or Grace or even Prudence. But we know when we have enough (Prudence is borderline). Some nineteenth century novelists liked to give their characters very obvious names; but you have to go back a long way before you find Bunyan (for example) putting hands and feet on pure abstractions: Temptation, Despondency, and so on. What I want to say now is this: we do it all the time! We do it in our minds. We put others in categories – we see them as categories – and they do the same with us. So inescapably are we fixed in those categories that we might as well have them branded across our foreheads. I have experienced being imprisoned in categories, and I confess that I have done the same to others. So and so is an angry man, I believe; so when I meet him I watch like a hawk for signs of it; and if he behaves gently I say to myself, 'See how well he conceals his anger!' How is that so very different from calling him Anger?

In meditation you take things out of their categories, their boxes. Or at least you lift the lids a little. You look at things in their starkness. (What other words might you use? Nakedness, facticity, *haecceitas*, 'suchness'.) In doing so, you do something similar for yourself; you escape to the same degree from your own box. You lift the lid a little. The feeling is of a world falling down, but you hear no crash. Death must be like that. Everything becomes clean. You lose the wish to talk and explain things to yourself.... Then the lid comes down again.

In Manila I felt like liberating those three convent sheep, but in fact they were doing it quite successfully themselves by their behaviour. Human beings are often far more sheepish.

Incompleteness

In our incompleteness we are close to God. The Scriptures tell us that 'the Lord is close to the broken-hearted.' It does not follow that if you want to be near the Lord you must be brokenhearted; but you do have to be open hearted. To be open is to be incomplete.

Imagine a completed circle, with no chink in its circumference. Everything on the inside remains sealed inside, and the outside cannot penetrate. The living creatures we share the world with are like that: their natures are somehow complete. Birds build their nests the same way, century after century; whatever changes we see in animal behaviour are negligible compared to human change. We human beings are like a circle with an incomplete circumference; what is inside can flow out, and the whole world can flow in; everything becomes possible. That chink in our armour makes us capable of the infinite. It is therefore to be cherished, it is to be kept clear, however strong the temptation to settle for less, to close down and be comfortable like the animals.

How we crave to close the circle, to be complete! We would use anything whatsoever to exclude the draught from beyond, from the infinite; we would fill our lives with things, experiences, travel, distractions, entertainment, loves and friendships (we are even capable of using people as draught-excluders). We use anything we can find to fill the gap. None of these, we know, not even love, can exclude the draught forever.

We have moments when all our draught-exclusion comes apart. We feel empty, and it is a painful experience. It is 3 p.m. on your day off and you don't know what to do with yourself. Or it is an ordinary day and everyone else seems so engrossed, but you feel no will to do anything or to go anywhere, to read a book or listen to music. So you eat! You fill your stomach, but your heart remains empty. You could have done worse: you could have taken to the drink, which is what many do. But neither of these ways is a solution.

There is no solution. Perhaps this is because there was no problem, for a start. We create a problem out of something that was not itself a problem. In trying to flee from the experience of openness – that chink in the armour – we create problems for ourselves. The real problem is not the openness but our fleeing from it. It is no solution to find a new way of fleeing. Instead we must stop fleeing and go back.

To do this is to meditate. It is possible, of course, to turn even meditation into a way of filling the gap, but meditation itself will show us this if we practise it. To meditate in the right spirit is to sit quietly in the presence of God in our incompleteness. Our very incompleteness is our most original prayer. Don't try to fill that empty space with words or forced feelings. Leave it as it is. Forget about yourself and your need to feel complete. You do this by focusing your attention on God. I know that this is not a clear instruction, because God is mysterious and beyond our focus. But as we can know about (and sometimes sense) the presence of a person whom we cannot see, we know about (and sometimes sense) the presence of God; this is enough. Don't try and wind yourself up into high feelings: that would probably be just another attempt to close the circle. Yes, we are capable, as I said, of using even meditation and prayer to exclude God.

After half an hour or so of this, you may have nothing much to report. It is quite possible that you were just sleeping and moping. Don't be shocked; it was not the first half-hour that you ever wasted in your life! But you don't even have the satisfaction of being sure that you wasted it! However, you know this much: even if you wasted the time, that would not be as bad as insulating yourself in a cocoon of superior feelings. It is also quite possible, of course, that you were really holding your spirit in its incompleteness before God.

Freedom

I knew a woman who kept the ducklings housed until they were fully grown. Then one fine Spring day she decided to let them out. She opened the door, expecting them to come half-running half-flying out, as ducks do when they are in a hurry. Instead they held their station. She went in and tried to shoo them out, but they avoided the open door like the mouth of hell. Freedom is much more frightening than captivity. Not only ducks but we ourselves know that. 'See how peacefully captured criminals sleep.'

Sartre made absolute freedom his theme. A human life, he said (in other words), is like a spark of freedom moving through a dense world of solid objects. I can be free in the present instant as I perform some action, but in the next instant that action is fixed as in amber; it is fixed in the past, it has become like another solid object. Freedom is terrifying (as ducks will tell you); it is like stepping into the void. So we would like to steer clear of it altogether; we would like to be fixed and unfree like objects. Objects are very secure: they never have to take risks or make decisions, their feelings are never hurt, their plans never defeated, their ideas never rejected. Who wouldn't love to be an object at times?

Freedom, for Sartre, always meant separation from things, even separation from oneself. Freedom is in the present instant, the now, and everything that is not now is like a solid object, fixed, unfree. All customs, habits, organisations, traditions, laws, religions … all, all are attempts to avoid freedom and to turn oneself into a solid object. I know what you are wondering: who or what is this elusive 'I', this unattached self whose nature is freedom? Well, it is no thing, it is nothing. You are, he said, *néant*, nothing. You are separated from everything, so naturally you are nothing. As a nothing, you have no ties to anything, you are absolutely free. This heady doctrine, illustrated by Sartre in many novels and plays, drove a generation (or two) of young people crazy: from the 1940s to the 1960s.

I wonder if most of western philosophy isn't just degenerated theology? Could it be, for example, that Heidegger is just Eckhart without God, and Sartre St John of the Cross without God?

Sartre's philosophy certainly looks like a caricature of one part of Christian teaching about the spiritual life: how one has to be detached from things, and even from oneself. John of the Cross told us that we can expect to experience *nada*, nothingness. Even on the summit of Mount Carmel, he said, you will know *nada*. The Holy of Holies, the place of meeting with God, will be perfectly empty. The place to meet God is ever in emptiness, in freedom from things and from oneself. But in Christian spirituality we are to be detached from things out of love, not out of nausea. (*La Nausée* was the title of Sartre's first novel.) Love, in

Sartre's nightmarish vision, is the will to turn the other into an object. But among Christians, even the posters on the wall have it by now: 'If you love something set it free.' If you love a person you will not destroy that person's freedom; you will not treat him or her as an object, a possession. Love is unpossessive, 'does not seek its own.' And if you are detached from yourself it is not out of disgust and self-hatred, but in the astonishing freedom that you see in genuinely saintly people.

Why should Sartre or anyone think that simply disidentifying with everything will make you free? Why, because somewhere in his mind, I believe, a mechanical image was lurking. In reaction to his philosophy teacher he had a horror of fixed essences; I think he must have felt that they were somehow competing for his space. Billiard balls! To get away from them it is not enough to go into your mind – because you even produce these things yourself! You have to become *néant*. This is all reverse gear, no matter how heroic it is made to look.

A Christian becomes *néant* by embracing everything. Forward gear, no billiard balls. Plunge everything into the nothingness that is your being. If it really is nothingness it will never be soiled or destroyed. Thank God (that contradiction in terms, according to Sartre) there are different ways of being nothing.

Free as Naught is free

'In all you do, be as free of it as Naught is free, which is neither here nor there,' said Meister Eckhart. Don't turn over the page yet! It gets easier. It was one of his many strange sayings: strange but full of meaning, or rather, strange because full of meaning.

Imagine that you were a schoolchild in ancient Rome, and your homework was the following: multiply MDCCLXIX by XIV. How would you proceed? (It can be done, but it takes a couple of days!) The Romans got nowhere with mathematics because they were short one vital digit: 0. They were not stupid people; how did they miss such a simple thing? The simplest things, of course are the hardest to see, but once they are seen we wonder how anyone ever failed to see them. The Romans were practical people: '1' can refer to this thing, '2' to this and that, etc., but '0' refers to nothing. What is the use of such a digit? The answer is that it frees the whole number system from gridlock. It is like that yellow painted square you see at cross-roads; the rule says: don't stop in that square! In other words, keep it empty, keep it at 0; when it is equal to 0 the traffic is no longer gridlocked, it can move.

Or imagine the game in which there are little numbered or coloured pieces that can slide horizontally and vertically within a plastic frame. One space is empty, so that any of the adjoining pieces can move into it, leaving their own space empty as they do so. That one empty space is able to move all over the board. It sets each piece free to move when it comes near it. That wonderful digit '0' was an Indian invention which came into the West through the Arabs. That is why our numerals are called Arabic.

Listen now again to Eckhart: 'In all you do, be as free of it as Naught is free, which is neither here nor there.' Naught is neither here nor there, neither this nor that, as the ancient Romans would have agreed, had someone told them about it. It is free itself, and it sets everything else free. All the other digits are tied, so to speak; only naught is free. Naught can do its work and pass on, asking for nothing; it is not wishing to be 1 or 2 or any other number; it is not seeking gain. Our actions, said Eckhart, should have that quality.

There is usually a great deal of attachment in everything we do: we are attached to some reward, or to the idea of success, or to winning someone's admiration. Or more subtly, we have been doing this or that for years, so that it has become for us a symbol of the stability of the world. We are not free in it as Naught is free. We love someone, we say, but that could mean just about anything: lust, dependency, a need for excitement and distraction, a need to fill the mind, a flight from loneliness ... but perhaps often real love. We are not always free as Naught is free: looking for nothing ourselves, but helping to set the other free.

When you do something with no attachment but simply and naturally, like the apple falling from the tree, you know what freedom is: I don't mean freedom from external restraints, but the much more difficult freedom from the self-seeking self, the ego. How good it would be to die like the apple falling from the tree!

'o' even looks like nothing. It looks like a hole. It is a bit of emptiness. Emptiness is this freedom that Eckhart spoke of. There are many ways in which you might illustrate it for yourself, but when you get to know it closely it becomes its own illustration. If these can help to make the reality of it present to you as you sit in meditation, take your pick:

- A bowl is an emptiness, an invitation, a welcome. Before there were ceramic bowls, people no doubt used their cupped hands to drink from the stream. Many people, by some instinct, hold their hands in their lap in just this gesture when they pray.
- A window is an area of nothingness. Imagine a room with no windows! Meditation is a window. It is not absolute nothingness; it is a window.
- A wheel is useful, said an ancient Chinese sage, because there is an opening in the hub, into which an axle fits. If there were no opening, the wheel would be useless. There is no need to be afraid of emptiness: it can take us farther than all our firm plans.
- A flute is empty, not solid; solidity makes no music at all, only thumps and thuds.
- This one is your homework: invent your own image for meditation.

Solitude and interiority

She had some of the habits of an alcoholic, though she never touched a drop. She had friends stashed away in all kinds of places, so that she would never need to be alone. She came gushing at you, leaving you almost no freedom about being her

friend; she put you on, like a garment. She changed and wore her
friends like clothes, to hide the nakedness of her solitude. She
had an enormous turnover: her exuberant friendliness and her
attractive appearance won most people over in minutes. At the
moment they could not see behind her the long trail of abandoned friends, like empty bottles or clothes out of fashion. Her
main story, shared within minutes, was her abandonment by the
great love of her life: she had walked out on him, and he did
nothing to stop her. He had often been talking, she said, of his
need to be alone sometimes; this was sure proof that he was
falling out of love with her.... He had no solitude left, I thought
to myself, because it was all used up covering hers.

It was uncanny: she could read your feelings instantly. If your
mind wandered for a second, she would say, 'You're not here!'
or 'You've changed suddenly!' or 'You're bored with me!' This
gave a mistaken impression of depth; in fact she lived entirely on
the surface, at the level of the senses. Many animals, for the same
reason, have that ability – dogs, for instance. She gave little or no
evidence of interior life. Meeting her was a strange experience,
but it is always instructive to meet an extremist: bring your eye
back a certain distance along the line from that extreme, and you
see ... yourself.

Solitude and interiority. They are not words that suggest light
and joy; for many they suggest just the opposite, darkness and
sadness. But surely there are degrees of light and degrees of joy.
Light and joy can sometimes be very superficial; they can be
garish and cheap. But when we go a little below the surface they
begin to be different: deeper, quieter, more satisfying. When we
begin to love this quieter quality we are beginning to appreciate
solitude and interiority.

It is not a choice between inside and outside, between
interiority and making myself useful. People who can savour
solitude and interiority are not necessarily antisocial types who
care only about themselves. In fact I will have nothing to bring
to others unless I am able to enter my own solitude and
interiority; I will just be a taker, not a giver, I will use other

people as means of escaping from myself, I will use them like clothes.

What do I find, for myself and for others, when I am 'sitting on my own stem, like the plants,' as someone put it? For a start I discover that being human is not a matter of satisfying endless cravings that pull me around wherever they want, once I abandon myself to them. I can quite easily go behind them, where there is a deep calm. In a while, if I stay put, there is a sense of freedom and vastness. This is one of the places where I can become conscious of God's presence. Like the innermost part of the Temple in Jerusalem, where only the High Priest entered once a year, it is the 'Holy of Holies'. That part of the Temple used to contain the Ark of the Covenant and Aaron's rod, but by the Lord's time, these had been lost: the Holy of Holies was an empty space. I can meet God anywhere, but perhaps in a special way in that Holy of Holies, and I don't need to wait a year to go in there: I can go in at any time. All I need to do is sit upright in a quiet place and know the presence of God within me and around me. Then I let the noise of all my cravings pass over me like a storm and die away. I cannot tell what that Presence will do in the Holy of Holies: only God knows. I only need to be faithful to it.

Then when I go out from that holy place I will not be a beggar, a taker, a craver. Like Moses after his meeting with God, I may even shine a little.

Downwardly mobile God

Is God up- or downwardly mobile? We would like our God to be upwardly mobile, but it appears that God wants to be downwardly mobile. Our world wants to push God more and more into the cold heavens, away from life and life's real concerns, up into the blue, like a lost kite. But God, in Christ, has entered our world and lives among us. 'Though he was in the form of God, Jesus did not count equality with God a thing to be grasped. He emptied himself, taking the form of a servant, and became as human beings are … ' (Philippians 2:6-7).

Many people throughout the centuries went to extremes to find images for this upside-down God of ours. Hadewijch, a woman mystic of the early thirteenth century, wrote: 'There stood a tree with its roots upwards and its top downwards.… The Angel said to me: "Climb this tree from the beginning to the end, all the way to the profound roots of the incomprehensible God!"' Ruysbroeck in the fourteenth century also spoke of an upside-down tree. The seeker after God, he said, 'must climb the tree of faith, which grows downwards from above, since its roots are in the Godhead.' Strange language! Strange extreme of imagery, unconsciously echoing across ages and cultures the *Katha Upanishad*. But the cause of it all is our God's strange ways with us.

Degree zero. That is the promised land, the place where the true temple will rise, with its Holy of Holies stark empty. It is the object of all desiring, yet desire can never attain it, because to desire it is to risk making it a plaything for the ego. What? Are we saying it is impossible to desire God? I know it is normal to speak of desiring God. But that is highly ambiguous language. Among those who knew God best, some used the language of desire and others did not. St Catherine of Siena's writings are full of burning desire, while Eckhart could say, 'I pray God to rid me of God!' These two people belonged to the same century and the same Order, yet their expression is utterly different. I wonder how many of us could experience the desire that Catherine felt, and if we could, would we call it desire? How would it compare with the host of egocentric desires that have almost become the very identity of most people? But of course we could not feel it – unless we were Catherine of Siena. It needs a superhuman refinement of desire to desire God rather than just 'the things of God.' (Once, in an essay, a Polish student wrote, 'God and his things' – making the distinction much clearer than the standard phrase does.) Eckhart prayed God to rid him of God. That is, he prayed God to rid him of Eckhart's God. 'O God, you are my God,' we pray. But the danger is that *my* God might not be God.

No doubt God will educate our desires through the circum-
stances of our lives, if we don't resist. But there is still room for
the other way: degree zero. God is sure to be in the lowest place.
Go there and you will be in the presence of God. Degree zero is
meditation, the way of emptiness.

Hamadryads

Have you met any hamadryads lately? Any what? *Hamadryads*.
They are the spirits of trees. Each tree has its hamadryad, which
is born with it and dies with it. No, you say, I haven't met any
of them face to face, but I have felt that trees had something.

You are right, I think; and you are not the first to say so. I
don't imagine that the ancient Greeks were able to see hamadryads
either, but like you they felt something, and they gave it the
name 'hamadryad' (which comes from *hama* meaning 'together
with' and *drus* meaning 'tree'). Hamadryads continued to make
their presence felt for a long time, not only in Greek but in
English literature. Spenser, for example, wrote of 'the wooddy
nymphes, fair Hamadryades ... and All the troupe of light-foot
Naiades.' (The naiads did for water what the hamadryads did for
trees.) But as centuries went by, trees lost their spirits (by the
way, these spirits were feminine). Dr Johnson complained in
1769, 'Nothing has deterred these audacious aldermen from
violating the hamadryads of George Lane!' And in 1873 Lowell
wrote, 'I am not sure that the tree was the gainer when the
hamadryad flitted and left nothing but ship-timber.'

To change the subject (but you will see the connection), do
you remember *Little Big Man,* the book and the film? Do you
remember the ancient Indian chief who said (I'm quoting from
memory, so I'll be sparing with quotation marks): White men
think that everything is dead – rocks, trees, rivers, even people.
But Human Beings (his own tribe) know that everything is
alive.... The old man understood us very well. He didn't need
to know the figures: that seventy million people were killed in
battle or by extermination or bombing or in camps between 1914

and 1945 in Europe and Russia. He didn't need to foresee the firestorming of Dresden nor the 'defoliation' of Vietnam (which meant: burn everything). He didn't need to foresee the statistics of abortion. Yes, when White Men lose their religious beliefs they believe all the more fervently in death. The little hamadryads didn't stand a chance.

An Oxford scholar, E.B. Taylor, introduced the word 'animism' into English in 1866, in an article entitled 'The Religion of Savages'. 'The theory which endows the phenomena of nature with personal life might perhaps be conveniently called Animism,' he wrote. This was a primitive form of religion, he said, an early phase in its evolution (he was writing only seven years after the publication of Darwin's *Origin of Species*). The more evolved religions, he said, overcome animism to a greater or lesser extent, placing a Supreme Spirit entirely outside nature.

So, we ask in all simplicity, is nature therefore sucked entirely dry of spirit? Is everything dead, as the Chief said? Is all personhood devoured by God? Were those fierce atheists right who said that God is the best part of ourselves (and the world) projected, sent off into outer space? Or the smoother ones who say the same thing in gentle psychotherapeutic language, are they right? Or the New Age devotees who dance again around the tree, pretending to know what the druids thought and felt, are they right ... ? If God is dead, yes they are right.

But to believe in the Creator God is to see everything, every stick and stone, every tree and river, every human being, as a gift. There could be no stronger basis for a gracious attitude to the world. One's whole life becomes thanksgiving.

> I thank you God for most this amazing day,
> for the leaping greenly spirits of trees,
> for a blue true dream of sky,
> for everything that is positive that is natural that is yes.
>
> (e.e. cummings)

Every creature is a gift of God and speaks of its Giver. If I go to the heart of the creature I will find God, for God is the deepest meaning of everything. Yes, I can sit under a tree and find the Presence there. We think of the presence of God in too general terms (maybe), as if God could be present only in things that were universal; and since the only universal things are thoughts, we are left with a God of thought alone.

But I want to discover the here and now God of my favourite tree. For years I have had a special name for that enormous lime tree that feels like a cathedral of nature. Till now I have told nobody that its name is Yugushama (it has to be pronounced slowly: 'yoogooshama'). I have never seen that word written till this moment. I didn't plan the name, but now that I look at it, perhaps the 'you' at the beginning is the need to see the tree as a presence; and (don't laugh) perhaps the 'goosh' is some kind of spirit! The leaping spirit of my tree, its hamadryad if you will, reaches up silently to the Creator God; it knows the ecstasies of full life, it agonises in storms, springs into new life, loses everything in the fall of the year. It is a place of meeting with God. Outer space is unimaginable, but my God lives here for me when I sit here, when I meditate here, when I fall asleep on the grass under its enormous branches. My God is not just a God who exists. My God lives.

SIX

The Way of Emptiness: 'Into Your Hands ... '

Questions, questions, questions!

What would life be like without the ego? Whose life? Ours, mine. But who are you? – No, I don't mean 'What's your name?' Your name is only an external label, and it's not even unique to you. When you were born you had no name; who were you then? Don't tell me you were the child of so and so, because that is only passing the question back to the generation before you. Who are you? You tell me you are a farmer or a nurse or a worker in such and such a place: that is only telling me what you do, but what I want to know is who you are. (Are my questions annoying you?)

Now take your wife: who is she? 'She's my wife!' But she was not always your wife; who was she before she married you? And did marrying you change her identity? It may have changed her name, yes, but as I said, a person's name does not tell you who he or she is. And you, Mrs, who is your husband? And who are your children?

What is there when you lift the names off things and people? (As Dennis the Menace asked his mother, 'Why do I ask so many questions?')

Are these questions answerable in the way I put them? No, I don't mean, Are they difficult to answer? I mean, Can they be answered at all? A name expresses a relationship, and if I exclude relationship am I not emptying the name of its meaning? Who would you be if you were unrelated to anyone or anything? – if you were unique and solitary and undescended from anyone? You would be nameless, would you not? And for the best of reasons: you would not and could not exist. (Are you still with me?)

Now God is unique and undescended, and ultimately name-less, the mystics tell us; so ... does God exist? (I'll let you off the hook with this question for the moment.)

Have you ever wondered what the '-el' means at the end of some names? Daniel, Michael, Raphael, Gabriel ... or some-times the '-el' is at the beginning: Elizabeth, Elijah, Elisha. It is short for *Elohim*, a Hebrew name for God. Some names, then, directly express a relationship with God. We might think of all names as doing that, even if not explicitly. A person's deepest identity is his or her relationship with God. Your surname expresses your kinship with thousands of people; you can think of your first name as expressing your kinship with God: 'I have called you by your name, you are mine.' (It's now a while since I asked you a question.)

Coming back to God, who is unique and undescended from any line, does God therefore have no relationships? How could we forget? The Trinity! God is all relationship! The Divine Persons, we are told, are 'constituted' by their relationships with one another. What does this mean? The Father does not *have*, but *is*, a relationship to the Son; and the Son *is* a relationship to the Father; and the Holy Spirit *is* the relationship between them. Supremely in the Trinity we see that persons are relationships.

What is a question? How is a question different from an answer? A question is a kind of opening. If a question is a door opening, an answer is a door closing. Which do you prefer, questions or answers? – open doors or closed? Well, if you are like the rest of us, you will say that sometimes you prefer one and sometimes the other. When do we close doors? Isn't it when we feel cold, or unsafe, or unwilling to be on call or on view? If you were feeling warm and safe and communicative, would you not prefer the door open? There are persons who are like open doors, and there are others who are like closed doors. The open ones are like questions: knowing their own incompleteness, they are receptive, eager, alert, also humble and outward-looking. The ultimate openness is the openness to God, who is open to us; we always have a question for or about God. Would it not be a shame to take the edge off that question? – to settle into our private selves, cold, fearful, solitary, unreceptive, unavailable, inward-looking?

So why have I been asking you so many questions? Because I've been wondering if one can live like a question. Because 'Question' is your name, or rather your identity! I've been trying to touch your identity. I've been trying to find out who you are ... haven't I?

Humility

If you hear of a saint who had to struggle to be humble, you can be quite sure that it was no saint but a hypocrite. Such people have often been held up for our admiration. But just think: if you met some people who were 'struggling' to make themselves believe that 2 + 2 = 4 you would be certain that they were completely innocent of mathematics. Humility is truth, it has always been said; and one either sees a truth or one does not. If people are only 'struggling' to see it, they do not see it. If they are struggling to be humble they are by that very fact proving themselves proud. Instead of coming out and saying, 'I'm a proud man, I'm a proud woman,' (which would be true, and the truth might set them free) they tell us they are struggling to be humble. Forgive my saying so but they are no saints.

What reputed saints say about humility is a reliable test of their sanctity. A preacher was once heard to announce, 'It is my humility that makes me the man I am.' The original meaning of *humility* is an objective state, not something in your mind, not an attitude. We use the word in this sense when we say that someone has 'a humble position'. The word comes from *humus*, the Latin word for 'earth'. If you are close to the ground, close to the bottom, you are humble, no matter what your attitude is. But the attitude soon becomes the principal thing, and we would like to be seen as 'humble' – not, mind you, objectively lowly or close to the bottom, but rather right up there as far as possible, looking down, yet acting as if we were still down here. You guessed: it is principally for the eyes of others. (If we succeed in fooling others, then we may be able to fool ourselves a little too: this is the way with many 'attitudes'.) We would like others to observe the vast difference there is between our actual greatness and the humble opinion we have of ourselves. The greater the distance the greater we will seem in their eyes: 'all that and so humble too!' In reality, the more humble the less! A cultivated humility has its exact opposite built into it in this way. It is only in a real saint that you see real humility; all the rest is done with mirrors.

You don't need to cultivate humility, you need to search for the truth. The truth will make you truthfully humble, so much so that you will not even be tempted to talk about humility any more. The deepest truth about you is not your position on the social ladder but your relationship to God. If that relationship has struck into your heart, then you will know how to relate truthfully to God and to others, without a cultivated 'humble' attitude.

One morning about 850 years ago St Bernard was preaching to his monks after some crisis had shaken the community's confidence. He said, 'We can breathe again, my brothers, for even if we are nothing in our own hearts, perhaps there is another opinion of us hidden in the heart of God.... Before God we may be nothing, but within God we are something.' We do not have to (we cannot) stand over against God, perhaps thinking that if we act humble enough we will get God's attention. We exist within God, whether we are great sinners or saints or anywhere in between. That is our dignity and it does not depend on us. It is ours no matter what we do, it can never be taken away from us. All creatures are 'poured out from God and yet remain within,' said Meister Eckhart. That is a strange saying, yet we can understand it. If you pour water out of a jug it is poured out and no longer remains within; but if you pour out your knowledge, or your love, it is poured out and yet it remains within you; it is not separated one millimetre from you. God poured us out in creation but we remain within, we are not separated from God.

When the truth of this strikes into your heart you will not have to go begging to others for some good opinion of yourself, you will not be deeply affected by praise or blame, you will not have to cultivate any 'attitude', especially not false humility. You will be able to act directly and simply in all things, for you will know at one and the same time your greatness and your nothingness, and for the first time there will be no conflict between these: they will be unshakeable truths, they will be the north and south poles of your existence.

The way of emptiness

It was a voice back from the grave. The familiar play of words, the tone of voice, the accent, the freshness that his mind gave to every topic: all were there, as when the living voice was heard two years before. He was a good friend for many years, a priest, a very human being; his early death was like the death of a brother.

Past and present hovered around each other in a strange dance as the tape played, moved through each other, changed places and returned to the beginning. It was a great sadness to know that there was nothing now but these tapes; no rerun would ever produce the slightest variation till Kingdom come. All was fixed forever in the past, though one seemed to be listening to the living man who made words a continual surprise.

He was speaking to a group of people, identified only as coughs and shuffles and an occasional faintly heard question. You heard him turn pages, you noticed a slight hesitation, you picked up signals that they probably did not. These marks on magnetic tape would survive, but their source had vanished forever.

'Though he was in the form of God, Jesus did not count equality with God a thing to be grasped. He emptied himself, taking the form of a servant, and became as human beings are ...' (Philippians 2:6-7). Then the hesitation, and then he said: I find

this totally fascinating ... the self-emptying of God, the poverty
of Christ. It has nothing much to do with goods; it's about the
way he was. Christ's way of being about the place was the human
way.... He revealed the Father more by his being – his humanly
being – than by anything else; then secondly by his doing, and
only then by his saying. He came bodily among us, he pitched
his tent down here, and that says something mighty about who
God is. 'And being found in human form, he humbled himself
and became obedient unto death, even death on a cross.' The
way of emptiness, he said (hesitating again, for this was a new
awareness in his own life), the way of nothingness is God's way
with us. I think of him lying in his grave. I missed his funeral, I
was at the other side of the world, I didn't know for weeks that
he was dead. Being found in human form he became obedient
unto death. The Almighty God's way with us is the way of utter
powerlessness. It took the disciples a long time to see that about
Jesus: as late as Gethsemane Peter knocked off your man's ear
with a good shot; he still didn't know that that wasn't Jesus's way
of going about things. And the sheer loneliness of his passion....
When you're going through something you can say: At least
those people out there understand me. But they were nowhere
in sight; they were gone, *cosa in áirde*, and they came back only
when he was dead.

Death is our final poverty. It is our powerlessness, our
emptiness. We too are found in human form and have to be
obedient unto death. The years pass swiftly and we are gone, our
life is over like a sigh. The living walking person disappears and
leaves only fixed traces behind; he or she has vanished into God.
It cannot be easy to vanish. We will have to know in our own
bodies and souls the self-emptying of God, the powerlessness,
the nothingness; otherwise we will have no inkling of who God
is. The weakening body, the faltering of belief in oneself, the
humility of being in the end a merely human being: that will be
able to tell us something mighty about God. And it won't be just
the telling, it will be the doing ... and the being.

Beautiful candles of belief

'The beautiful candles of belief, that would not do to light the world any more, they would still burn sweetly and sufficiently in the inner room of his soul and in the silence of his retirement.' It is D.H. Lawrence describing the faith of an elderly gentleman in his novel, *Women in Love*. In that one beautiful sad sentence Lawrence expressed the double alienation in western culture: alienation from community and from the life of the body. Many writers have drawn attention to these. They are a withdrawal into the self, and even further, into the psyche: in Lawrence's language, 'retirement' (from public life, community) into 'the inner room of his soul' (his psyche). They are symptoms of some great defeat. Lawrence wrote early in this century. By the middle of the century Wittgenstein had spent his mature years attempting to cure western culture of this double alienation: from the terrible introversion of 'the inner life' and an equally terrible individualism. Fergus Kerr writes that Wittgenstein's effort was 'to retrieve the natural expressiveness of the human body, and to reaffirm ... community.'

To test the water I raised this question with a group of ordinary Catholics whom I meet regularly for discussion. 'Let's try an experiment,' I said; 'I will defend a certain position, and you can floor me! Let's have a fierce debate!' They were all for it. I then began to express in a pure form the double alienation in our modern world, and the way it is when it becomes religious: 'What matters is the inner life. The outer life is of no account. The world is but a source of temptation. Only in the depths of our heart can we meet God. (And quoting a leaflet I remember from childhood), "Remember, man, thou hast but one soul to save; and after that the Judgment." ' And more to that effect. Then I waited for the assault ... and waited ... but they all agreed with every word I said!

'What about the Christian teaching that God is everywhere, not just in the depth of your soul?' I said. 'What about St Paul's teaching that far from having only one soul to save, "we are all members of one another?" What about the sacraments? Are they not visible and public acts? What about *ex opere operato* … ?' Oops, sorry! Jargon! But what a truth that Latin tag expresses! Let me explain.

In the administration of the sacraments, the essential is what the priest does (provided he has the intention of doing what the Church intends), not how he is in his own inner life. This may sound mechanical and unspiritual. Surely, you say, the priest should be in the state of grace when he administers a sacrament. Of course he should. But supposing he is not? Who is to know? If the validity of a Mass depended on the inner state of the priest, you would never be certain that what you attended was a real Mass. Nor could you be certain that you were validly baptised. In other words, you could not be sure that you were a Christian. Nor could the priest be sure that he was a priest, or sure that he was a Christian. Nor could you be sure that anyone else was a Christian. In other words, the Church would be entirely invisible! Therefore it is just as important to believe in the outer life as it is to believe in the inner. The sacraments make use of material things: water, bread, wine, oils … and something bodily is done to you by other people: something (a) bodily, and (b) by other people. The beautiful candles of belief are lighted not only in 'the inner room of your soul' and in 'the silence of your retirement,' but publicly, visibly, and in the hands of the people standing around you, the Christian community. This community prays that the light of faith in you will light up the world.

The most intractable of all egos is the pious one: nothing can buffet it, because it claims nothing less than divine sanction. It usually just repeats the prejudices of the day (or the day before), and covers them with a protective coating of religious feeling and language. One eye looks in and the other looks up, as with the citizens of Laputa, whom Gulliver met on his travels. (Swift was striking at the rationalists of his day: Laputa, I imagine, is *La puta*, a reference to Luther's calling reason 'a whore'.) There is a kind of spirituality that follows the same lines, escaping inwards and upwards. I recall a text in Eckhart where he advises us to be very careful of the words 'in' and 'up'. They very easily become a denial of community and a denial of the body.

An hour later I was still defending myself against charges of heresy! That private, inner, other-worldly, 'ghostly' kind of spirituality takes a long time to die. I remember hearing a very old version of the Act of Contrition in the confessional once: '... and to you, my ghostly father.... ' It gave me a slight shiver, because it is now several years since we began to say Holy Spirit for Holy Ghost. A ghostly father must be a spiritual father, but that was not the first thing I thought of; the first thing was that I was wearing my Dominican habit, which is white! Perhaps in future I should wear the other part of it more often, the black part. Black is not an up-and-in colour; it is down-and-out colour. Black like the good earth.

The whole apple

There on the table is an apple. Someone comes up and says, 'Oh, here is an apple! Let me tell you about it. It has two sides: an inside and an outside, and the essence is the inside, the "inner life" of the apple. The outside is much less important and you cannot put much trust in it. Concentrate on the inside and you will understand all about the apple.' You say, 'Rubbish!' Then the person goes away and tells everyone that you are denying the existence of the insides of apples. Rubbish! You are denying the value of the distinction between insides and outsides, and that's a different matter altogether. For 'apples' say 'human beings', and now you're talking. We did indeed put such emphasis on the inner life (we also called it the spiritual life) that we seemed to be making light of the outer life; and then when we begin to stress the importance of the outer life we appear to some to be denying the inner. It is useful, I think, to reflect on this.

Consider infant baptism. There are some Christian groups that disagree with it, but in the Catholic Church it is the normal practice. We bring the baby along, hoping it will sleep through

the whole ceremony! (To facilitate this, we even arrange to have
the baptismal water at body temperature.) What is said and done
there is said and done by adults; the baby is passive. But, you may
ask, how could anyone become a Christian while sound asleep?
And even awake, the baby couldn't care less about baptism.
Now, what about his or her inner life? Well, that baby has an
outside – not a very extensive one yet, but a real outside. And
inside and outside, in any case, are not like two separate worlds.
There is only one baby, for God's sake, and this is it. To say that
babies cannot be Christians is to say that being a Christian is a
matter of thinking, consciousness, awareness, decision.... It is
like saying that you cannot be a Christian while you are asleep.
Consider the consequences of thinking that way. If you die in
your sleep, is yours a Christian death? Or if you die in a coma,
are the sacraments they administer to you futile? And what about
all the times in your life you have not been fully conscious,
aware, and so on (all the times you fell asleep at prayers, or when
you were sick), were you a Christian then? Of course you were!
And if you die in your sleep, yours is a Christian death. So if you
were baptised as an infant, that was your first lesson that the
Christian faith is not something of your own devising. 'This is
the love I mean,' wrote John, 'not our love for God but God's
love for us,' and 'God loved us first.'

In fact all the sacraments, not only baptism, are seen as
moments of grace (a word that means 'gift'). Something is done
for you: people pour water over you, or they rub you with oil, or
feed you, or lay their hands on your head, or say words over you
... (in the case of marriage it is you who say the words, but the
presence of other people, to listen and watch, is regarded as
essential). In other words, there is a full recognition of you as a
bodily being: the Church does not see you just as an 'inside', an
interior and solitary ghost; it sees you whole. It is obliged to tell
you that God loves all of you, not just your brain-waves.

All of this should give us some indications about prayer. I met
a very earnest Christian who said he was allergic to Our Fathers
and Hail Marys and Grace before and after meals. Or rather he

was allergic to the way other people said them. He said that all prayer should be quiet and thoughtful, deep and heartfelt. This is a lofty ideal, and no one could ever pull it down, but I feel there has to be room for other kinds of prayer too. We are not always quiet and thoughtful, and if we prayed as if we were, it might be very forced and even hypocritical. There's a place for what you might call encrusted prayer: prayers that have become quite habitual. We are not always tender shoots and delicately open-ing buds; I often feel more like a tuft of scutch-grass or a piece of dried bark. There's a place for repetitive prayer, Hail Marys, Our Fathers and Graces, at whatever speed. There's a place for regular prayer: prayers on a timetable, and not just when one feels 'moved'. There's a place for not feeling so 'inward' and precious all the time. In other words, there's a place for all of us, in both senses: all of us together, and all of each person, inside and outside – the whole apple.

Inside and out

There is a restaurant in Rome where everything is inside out. When you go in you see a street scene: doors with numbers and letter boxes, street lamps, balconies, windows as seen from the outside with curtains and inner lights and with window boxes; there are even a few traffic signs.... It is very ingenious, but faintly disturbing: the body doesn't know whether to adjust to the interior or the exterior. Italians seem to have no problem with it, because they are accustomed to eating outdoors, but northern Europeans make a very great division between insides and outsides. In the tropics I had the same feeling about such 'indoor' things as pendulum clocks and desk telephones: they looked so out of place on the outside of a building! But you don't have to travel far to see such things: look over people's country hedges at home and you may see an old-fashioned bellows or a crane with hangers, changed from domestic use to garden ornament, still black but not with soot, unexpectedly clean and in the way, like old men retired from dirty jobs. There is a special

sadness about this kind of garden ornament: our own intimate
past is being hauled out shamelessly into public view, and it
begins to feel foreign even to ourselves. Still ... the answer
cannot be to bury oneself in the interior world. All that lies
hidden will be revealed, we are promised, will step out into
aletheia, into the bracing truth.

A friend told me this: I once knew a young woman, an only
child, who lived with her parents in a house surrounded by dense
growth, like a jungle. There were trees, high hedges, neglected
flowers and tangles of briars; there were also two ferocious dogs
to protect the sanctity, or whatever, of that inner place. When
I visited (which meant shouting from the gate), the hall-door
opened one inch, but there was no sound. I shouted some more,
asking for the young lady, who after all had sent for me. A flat
voice said, 'She's out,' the crack was closed and I was left
forgotten among the lilies, the brambles and the savage dogs. I
begin to understand now (he said) why she always seemed to be
wearing two or three cardigans and a couple of coats: they are a
well-insulated family, everything is on the inside.

Insides and outsides: these attach to the parallel needs that
normal people have, the need to be alone and the need to be with
others, to be hidden and to be visible, perhaps the need for
darkness and the need for light. May I ask naively, Where is
God? We say God is everywhere. That means inside and outside.
But it is not an easy thing to balance these: we are all asymmetri-
cal in this matter. Nowadays we find it easy enough to believe
that God is within us, so we say. But it is fatally easy to place God
in one's own interior in order to avoid God! It is one of the most
puzzling things we do in this age. My religion is my own
business, people tell you. It means: I want nothing to do with
your outside God, I don't want to hear any claims or demands,
or indeed any instruction, I reject your God in the name of God.

But can we divide God like that? If we do, then we are like that
family peeping suspiciously through the crack and closing
ourselves to everything that lies beyond. But God cannot be the
enemy of God. The God who lives within is the same God who

lives beyond my horizons and who calls me constantly into deeper and wider worlds.

If many people take flight into themselves it must be for good reasons, and the modern world offers us new ones every day. We need even better reasons to persuade us to come out again! It would not be enough to be told, 'It's healthy to get out of yourself.' We need a ravishing vision that will transport us beyond ourselves, a vision large enough to embrace private and public. We have a thirst for the beyond, for what is called 'transcendence'. We are capable of hearing and embracing the truth.

What makes us cower inside ourselves? Many things, I'm sure, but perhaps fear, most of all. Many people may be in flight from a God who is seen as purely 'outer', imposed and imposing, cold and judgmental, inspiring fear rather than love. We need to know that this God too is a caricature: not God at all. The God we worship is not one who drags out our inner life shamelessly, who turns our life inside out so that we have nowhere to hide and cannot escape. Our God is the deepest source even of our inner life, our intimacy. Our God embraces both worlds, the inner and the outer, and therefore makes it possible to move from one to the other. The God we know in intimacy is the Lord of heaven and earth.

Stepping out

'The whole creation prays,' wrote Tertullian in the third century. 'Cattle and wild beasts pray, and bend their knees, and in coming forth from their stalls and lairs look up to heaven, their mouth not idle, making the spirit move in their own fashion. Moreover the birds taking flight lift themselves up to heaven and, instead of hands, spread out the cross of their wings, while saying something that may be supposed to be a prayer.'

This may sound a little strange, somewhat pagan, to Christian ears. It reminds you of the American Indian who said that the birds build their nests round, just like the tents the people live in, 'because theirs is the same religion as ours.' Yet there is a whole Christian literature on this theme. If you were making a collection, you would have to include St Francis's *Canticle of the Sun* and de Chardin's *Hymn of the Universe*, and you could reach back to the book of Daniel for the Canticle in chapter 3.

What is this? – birds and cows saying their prayers, the sun moon and stars blessing God? Strange.... But the alternative is more strange. The alternative is to think that the human spirit is isolated from the rest of reality, a lonely spook that cannot identify with anything or feel at home in the world. That is the way to madness. If you want to see how we depend on the rest of creation, try depriving your fine mind of oxygen for a couple of minutes, or that stomach of yours of food for a few days.... How humiliating for the ego!

We are part of all creation. 'All creatures reach up to God through me,' said Eckhart. This was a familiar theme. We have something of all creatures in us: we are mineral, vegetative, animal and spiritual. If you cannot feel 'spiritual', then feel like an animal or a vegetable or a mineral; these are all decent creatures, and free of ego. If you feel hard and cold one day, just be a rock! Join all the other rocks that make up the building you are in; join all the rocks in the whole world! – 'you mountains and hills, O bless the Lord!'

Walking in the dark

Blindness is the ultimate form of darkness. It is darkness that you carry around with you, so there is no escape from it. We, sighted people, have only a very faint idea of it, no doubt. How vulnerable a blind person must feel! Imagine the danger of tripping at every step. I read of people blind from birth who received sight by implant, in their adult years, and who found at first that they could manage better without it. But for people who lost their sight, there must be very great suffering, a profound sense of helplessness. Sight is like feelers that can extend to any distance; you can plan your next move and the moves after it, almost automatically, you can get your bearings, you can take your place with confidence in the world. But close your eyes and walk around the room for two minutes! That is the most familiar place in the world to you, but look how strange it has become: you can 'see' no further than your fingertips, you seem to have diminished. Sight carried you to the horizon, but blindness reduces you to your mere self.

Bartimaeus was blind and lived by begging; he spent his days stretching out his hands into the darkness in the hope of receiving enough to live on till tomorrow, which would be just like today. When he heard that Jesus was passing by he began to shout, 'Have pity on me!' People told him to shut up, he was making too much noise. But he shouted all the more. 'Call him,' Jesus said. 'Cheer up!' they told him. 'On your feet, he's calling you' (Mark 10:49). Then, the account continues, 'throwing his cloak aside, he jumped to his feet and came to Jesus.' He came, of course, still in the dark. It is a very powerful symbol of the life of faith: he walked in the dark. Did you notice that he threw his cloak aside? It was a strange thing for a blind person to do: would he find it again? Blind people have great trouble finding things, they need the world to stay put. See how carefully they place things, caressing them almost. But sighted people are forever throwing things around. Clearly, in throwing his cloak aside, Bartimaeus acted like a sighted man.

Faith is a kind of knowledge, yes, but it is dark knowledge. Still, this dark knowledge sets us free, somehow, to move with confidence. How good it would be to move without timidity, to travel through our life with freedom and joy, careless of all the petty matters that consume people's energy! We have dreams of the perfect way to live: to be rich in what matters – faith, hope, love – confuting the gloomy predictions that are heard on every side, leaping ahead to grasp the essential, throwing aside what is of no account. A blind beggar shows us how. While all the sighted people held their cloaks and their possessions around them with careful fingers, he alone leaped up, threw aside his cloak and ran to meet the Lord.

Another scene: this time in St John's Gospel. An official approaches Jesus in Cana, saying that his son is sick in Capernaum, twenty miles away. 'Sir, come down before my child dies,' he begged. Jesus said to him, 'You may go. Your son will live.' 'The man took Jesus at his word and departed' (John 4:50). Think yourself into his mind as he set out on the long journey. He had nothing concrete to rely on. He had only the stranger's word. But he started to walk and did not turn back. The writer of the Gospel, who put nothing in by chance, is telling us that our journey is no different; we have the word of Jesus to rely on, and nothing else.

Nothing else?

Nothing. The other things with which we surround the word of Jesus add nothing to it: buildings, organisations, traditions.... These unfold the word of Jesus for us, the Word who is Jesus, but they add nothing to it.

Strange! you say; would it not be better if we had many things to reassure us? Would these not help us to rely on the word of Jesus?

No, they would not. Look at it like this: your wife tells you she loves only you; she gives you her word. You believe her, but just to help you believe her better you check with everyone and you get a private detective to shadow her! Does that help you to believe her even more? Of course not! You prove that you don't believe her at all. In the life of faith we put aside other assurances and set out on the road with nothing but the word of Jesus to rely on.

Is this the lonely conscience before God? Are you forgetting the place of the community, the Church?

All structures, including the Church itself, are means to the final realisation of the Kingdom of God. But the realised Kingdom, the Parousia, being delayed, there is the strongest temptation to put other things in its place, to see our temporal arrangements as Parousia, as definitive. Then we cannot understand why it all keeps falling apart! We struggle to gather everybody in, and fret to see them leave: so we flatter the young and take the old for granted, we lament what is happening and we look back in nostalgia to golden ages that never in fact existed. It is a lack of faith in the victory of Christ's resurrection

It is similar to the individual's longing for immortality while forgetting that it is the resurrection that grounds our faith. The Church playing Parousia is just like an individual playing God. No, we are not lonely consciences before God; we are a community of believers *in via*, not settled down: 'born anew to a living hope through the resurrection of Jesus Christ from the dead,' not fighting a losing battle against rust and moth.

In via, on the road: like the blind beggar and the man worried about his sick son. These, like their remote ancestor Abraham, and for the same reason, are heroes of faith. They did not come from powerful families, nor did they have any special education, nor were they remarkable in any other way. But they walked the way of emptiness.

Take up your cross

'I need to get off work early tomorrow,' she said to the principal. I was just an idle visitor in a busy school, so I stood aside and picked up a book. But the office was small and I was still within earshot. She was young, smartly dressed and business-like. I could not help hearing what she said next: 'My husband is being crucified in the afternoon, and I need to be around to see that he comes to no harm.' My eyes stared and my mouth fell open. The cartoons have it right: that is what total amazement looks like. In any foreign country, but especially in a very foreign one, you pre-set your mind to receive all kinds of signals that you could never receive at home; this is why it is good for you to travel! But this was outside my waveband. Then I thought she must be joking: jokes explain everything. I was going to join in the conversation with a story about the man to be hanged whose last words were, as he stepped onto the trapdoor, 'Are you quite sure this thing is safe?' But nobody was laughing, and the young woman continued in her business-like way. 'Last year too,' she said, 'he was crucified, and to console himself he got drunk afterwards and we had a terrible time with him. So I'd be glad of the afternoon free.' Her request was granted and she stepped out trimly, her business accomplished.

I didn't need to ask; I had question-marks all over me. 'Here in the Philippines,' the principal explained, 'some of us work even on Good Friday!' But, but ... !' I said. 'Oh, the crucifixion?' she said, 'that's just something they do here. There are always a few men who carry crosses in the procession and they get crucified for five or ten minutes. They get nailed to the cross all right, but the nails don't carry the weight; they have ropes. Her husband does it every year to atone for his drinking, but it only makes him worse!'

Thank God for absurdities, for humour, for things off the beaten track! They force you to think, to extend the range of your common sense, to stretch your mind just as you stretch out your hand to steady yourself.

Which cross are we asked to carry: our own or Jesus's? He did not say, 'take up my cross,' but 'take up *your* cross and follow me.' That young husband already had a heavy cross of his own to carry, and a daily crucifixion to suffer. Why should he imitate the suffering of Jesus when he already had plenty of his own? He showed some extraordinary quality, whatever its name, and people sometimes need to do the exceptional thing ... but if it only made him worse ... ?

'Take heed of how you ought to follow God's way,' said Meister Eckhart in the fourteenth century, a time that knew its excesses. 'If you find that your shortest way to God does not consist of many external works and great labours or mortifications (which, quite simply, are not so very important unless you are especially called to them by God and have the strength to perform them without damage to your spiritual life), and if you find that you are not like this, keep quite calm and do not let yourself be too concerned about it.... But now you may say: "Our Lord Jesus Christ always practised what was the very best, and it is always him that we should imitate." That is true. One ought indeed to imitate our Lord, but still not in everything he did. Our Lord, we are told, fasted for forty days. But no one ought to undertake to imitate this. Many of his works Christ performed with the intention that we should imitate him spiritually, not physically. And so we ought to do our best to be able to imitate him with our reason, for he values our love more than our works.'

Eckhart has such sound common sense that I hope you will forgive me if I quote further. It is, as I say, like reaching out one's hand to steady oneself. About the ego's temptation to do big dramatic things, he said: 'It is sometimes harder for you to suppress one word than to keep completely silent. It is harder to endure one little word of contempt ... than to suffer a heavy blow for which you had steeled yourself. And it is much harder to be alone in the crowd than in the desert. And it is often harder to give up some little thing than something really big, harder to carry out a trifling enterprise than one that people think much more important.'

We don't need to be crucified every Good Friday, but the ego is called to die every day. Still, the cross of Christ and our own crosses go far beyond all the common sense in the world, beyond the wisdom of the Greeks (and the Germans). The Filipino people are to an extraordinary degree *maka-Diyos* (God-oriented) and at the same time *maka-tao* (people-oriented). They have none of that religious elitism that has so beset the west. They teach you to carry your cross any way you can.

Two thieves

I asked a group of people to make their own crosses in clay. No, they were not to be ornaments. And no, they were not to be crucifixes: that's Christ's cross, and he did not say, 'Take up my cross,' but 'Take up your cross.' Your cross will look very different from his. It is his that gives meaning to yours, true, but they will still look very different: you are being battered, like everyone else, but you are not being crucified. So make a symbol of your suffering....

Some of the group were puzzled by this, but crosses can be expected to puzzle, and not only puzzle but threaten to destroy. Still, they went to work, and within half an hour we had twenty different 'crosses', and some in the group began to talk about what they had made. One woman had begun by making a path with many obstacles on it: rough lumps of clay, large and small. The path was her life; the lumps were the many family troubles she had. Then, she said, she had got rid of the path and left just the obstacles! – because she suddenly saw that the obstacles were the path.

Many had made human figures, mostly in attitudes of prostration. Whether these represented themselves or a husband or wife or child, they were not saying. Nor did anyone push them to say; some things are so close and so painful that they are not ready for words. Speaking from a respectful distance we can say: your cross is first of all yourself. Take up your cross means: stagger onto your feet and try to walk. Jesus was nailed hands and feet to the cross. Your hands are your power to do things; your feet are your freedom to go places. Your cross is whatever immobilises you and takes your power away. Your cross is also the people you love most (people you hate are just an inconvenience). Their cross is yours because you love them. And so St Paul can seem to contradict himself in the space of a few verses; in Galatians 6:2 he said 'Bear one another's burdens,' and in 6:5 he said 'Each one will have to bear his or her own burden.' Your cross is yourself and more than yourself. Your cross is the way out of yourself, it is the death of the ego.

Another woman, with apologies, produced not only one but two crucifixes. She had tried to avoid the crucifix because I had said they should, but it expressed her thought better than anything else. 'But why two?' someone asked. 'They are the two thieves,' she said, 'and both of them are me!' There are times when she is one and times when she is the other. Before, she was always the bad thief, complaining and blaming everyone. But as the years have gone by, she has become more aware of other people's suffering, and she has seen her own suffering join her somehow to Christ. She cannot explain it very well, she says, but whether you are the good or the bad thief you are suffering; and now, even though she thinks it may be wrong, she feels there's hope even for the bad thief. All suffering has meaning because of the death of Jesus, and since suffering really is an art, the poor bad thief cannot be blamed entirely. Who would not want to save his own skin? There is hope for us all, she said, and hope for each of us in our different stages of life. If the bad thief had lived long enough he might have become a good thief.

It is not as if we were alone against some superior force called the ego; God's Providence is working for us, God's grace is working in us.

I gave them homework: introduce the idea of resurrection into the figure you have made. But do not do it by adding more clay, nor by removing any, but only by reshaping what you have. Your resurrection will come from your cross, your whole cross and nothing but your cross, not from anywhere else. Your cross is your way to God; the promised new life will come from death and not from avoidance of death. This is the content of our faith. Your resurrection is made possible by the resurrection of Christ, but it is yours: it is yours as your cross is yours. Let us see in clay how you imagine it. Let us see the hope you live by. Take up not only your cross but your resurrection.

Lightly at last

I have an Indonesian friend who tells me that among her tribe in Sumatra, the Batak, there is a ceremony called *manulangi* at the deathbed of one's parents. Each one of the family offers some morsel of food, and then the dying father or mother speaks. The words are listened to with utter attention. These words, said my friend, are more than words; they are like things, they will last forever, they *are* the father and mother. Whenever there is a crisis in the family – a dispute, some uncertainty, a tragedy – these sacred words will be repeated again and again. They bind the family together, reaching through the generations, beyond death.

'Beyond death', 'lasting forever.' It is an edifying story, but why are you telling it to us now? Are you perhaps trying to crawl out of the water and drag yourself up the beach to dry land, on the far shore? Do you pretend to reach beyond time and change? Are you, too, proudly longing to be master of your fate and captain of your soul? Admit that you are dreaming about it! Once, you were persuading us to leap on the wave of transience, but now you are talking perilously about 'beyond death'. Perhaps you already see your frail deeds dancing in a green bay?

Dying is part of living, and so to love life is to love death too, in some sense. But no ... no, I am not tempted to claim a ground that is common to life and death, a neutral place beyond them from which to survey them both. I have no wish to betray our severe blessing. I leave you, thinking of the last crossed hill where you and I will lie lightly at last, as the poet said. 'Curse, bless me now with your fierce tears, I pray:' I have imagined no comfort or protection against death; like you, I know none.

All the beautiful people we have ever loved will die, and we will die on the same or the next wave. There is no specific against mortality; we are found in human form and we are obedient unto death. We must be swept clean, we must be made new, we must vanish into God, not into a superior version of ourselves. We must let God be God, and the resurrection be the resurrection, not a boring conclusion. The weakening body, the faltering of belief in oneself, the humility of being in the end simply a human being: that falls within our range. Beyond is the open sea, the unknown .... The whole heart, the whole soul, the whole strength, the whole mind, the stream, the swell of our existence says, 'I will go beyond my boundaries, I will be the sea!' But what is it like to hope for something that is not egocentric?

My God, I am ready to be reduced, to be chastened, perhaps in the end to be nothing, if only I can know you! No, more than myself, I want my friends to know you, my God, my God, why have you ... for you I long, for you my ... soul is thirsting; my body pines for you like a dry weary land without water; I gaze on you in the sanctuary, in the living eyes of my dearest friends. The deep community of death makes brothers and sisters of us all. We have words of meaning for one another, *manulangi*, and morsels of food. I accept my own mortality but my God! my friends' I cannot fathom, I cannot understand how such beautiful people can expire, I cannot see 'through their unseeing eyes to the roots of the sea.'

But whether or not I understand, my life is in your hands, O Lord. And theirs ...

Our life, our death, are in your hands....